Nicole + Vi

May you find peace
and joy in all you
do!

WHAT OTHERS ARE SAYING
ABOUT AMANDA MOTTOLA
AND THIS BOOK

"Amanda is an amazing inspiration for all of us in her commitment to growth while achieving success. Her unique experiences, coupled with deep insights, create a resource for those seeking to overcome challenges while challenging themselves and others to be the best they can be. This is a valuable read for everyone as we continue our collective and independent journeys toward personal and professional fulfillment."

— Salvatore F. Menzo, EdD, Superintendent of
Goodwin University Magnet School System

"Amanda is a determined woman who has set out to better understand life and how she can inspire others to succeed. *Learning as a Lifelong Journey* will inspire purposeful living in all who read it."

— Fernando Pfannl, Former Paraguayan Ambassador

"It's been an amazing experience to witness Amanda's growth as a businessperson, a mom, and someone truly dedicated to making a difference in this world. We are all fortunate to share in her unique observations and practical experiences by absorbing this comprehensive book!"

— Don Fertman, Subway Chief Development Officer (Retired)
and Phoenix Chairman of the Board

"As a proud lifelong learner myself, Amanda's approach to leadership resonates with me. In this book, you get to dig in on important topics like being vulnerable, being purposeful, embracing course correction, and more. Make sure your notebook is close by because you will be grabbing great actionable 'gems' along the way."

— Cortney Nicoleta, President & CEO of United Way of Rhode Island

"Finding your mission and purpose in life is something that we should all strive to achieve. What the world needs more of is amazing individuals like Amanda who guides others through life using the steps she has learned to better her own life. As a fellow coach, I am honored to call Amanda a friend and colleague. May this book inspire you to reach for the stars. Dream big; you will never be bigger than your dreams."

— Karen Dalton, Dare to Dream Ranch Executive Director

"Amanda Mottola has that rare gift of not letting anything stand in the way of creating her destiny on her terms. Despite questions about her past as an adopted immigrant child, she has overcome the odds, developed self-awareness and wisdom, and now shares her gifts to help make the world better for everyone she comes in contact with. *Learning as a Lifelong Journey* will have you embracing your own journey with renewed vigor and hope."

— Patrick Snow, Publishing Coach and International Bestselling Author
of *Creating Your Own Destiny* and *The Affluent Entrepreneur*

"I've known Amanda since her days as a college student and when she interned at the Greater New Haven Chamber of Commerce. It was obvious to me then that Amanda was a special person with talent, ambition, and a keen sense of how to bring people together. I had no doubt she would excel and accomplish so much for her and everyone around her. *Learning as a Lifelong Journey* is the well-thought-out collection of lessons that has shaped her life and is a must read."

— Anthony Rescigno, former president of Greater
New Haven Chamber of Commerce

"I so enjoyed reading about Amanda's amazing journey as a child adopted from Paraguay and her quest to learn the truth about her roots. I also admired how she used the challenges of being different from those around her while growing up to become someone who can see things with an exceptional perspective and is committed to creating changes for the better. *Learning as a Lifelong Journey* is a true gift to readers looking to make positive changes in their own lives."

— Tyler R. Tichelaar, PhD and Award-Winning Author
of *Narrow Lives* and *The Best Place*

"*Learning As A Lifelong Journey* takes the reader on a self-reflective, heart-warming, and extraordinary journey to help uncover your purpose in life. The author draws on her experiences with adoption, encouraging you to make a difference simply by being your authentic self. Her life lessons are a beautiful reminder that every decision has a ripple effect."

— Susan Friedmann, CSP and Bestselling Author of *Finding Your Riches in Niches: How to Make it BIG in a small Market*

"Amanda Mottola's *Learning as a Lifelong Journey* is a tour-de-force about how to find the truth about who you are and then step into becoming who you want to be. Not letting any form of adversity hold her back, Amanda has become an inspiration to others who may feel like outsiders, but are actually called upon to lead the way."

— Nicole Gabriel, Author of *Finding Your Inner Truth* and *Stepping Into Your Becoming*

LEARNING
AS A LIFELONG
JOURNEY

BEING YOUR LEADER
OVERCOMING YOUR FEARS
SUCCEEDING IN YOUR CAREER

AMANDA MARIE MOTTOLA

AVIVA
PUBLISHING
New York

LEARNING
AS A LIFELONG
JOURNEY

LEARNING AS A LIFELONG JOURNEY

Being Your Leader, Overcoming Your Fears, Succeeding in Your Career

Published by:
Aviva Publishing
Lake Placid, NY
(518) 523-1320
www.AvivaPubs.com

Amanda Mottola
(203) 535-5003
amanda@amandamottola.com
www.AmandaMottola.com

ISBN: 978-1-63618-173-8
Library of Congress Control Number: 2022901482

Editors: Tyler Tichelaar and Larry Alexander, Superior Book Productions
Cover Designer: Nicole Gabriel, Angel Dog Productions
Interior Book Layout: Nicole Gabriel, Angel Dog Productions
Author Photo: Ashley Richer Photography

Every attempt has been made to properly source all quotes.

Printed in the United States of America.

First Edition

2 4 6 8 10 12

DEDICATION

To my birth mother, Maria Edelmira Ocampo Ayala, for giving me the gift of life.

My mom and dad for adopting and raising me to be the woman I am today.

My brothers for being my protectors and loving me more than a boat.

My best friend, Eva, for being my co-captain since our Lauralton Hall days.

Peter, my husband, for being on board with my crazy, over-the-top ideas and dreams!

And last, but not least, to the loves of my life, Luca and Enzo, for making me the happiest mama alive, and to my future children. I love you!

This book is also dedicated to you, the reader. May it inspire you to dream big and change the world.

Besos y abrazos XO.

ACKNOWLEDGMENTS

Amy Neale—Thank you for continuing to believe in me and encouraging my entrepreneurial spirit through the growth of Otraway and this book.

Brian and Nate—You are the best brothers a sister could have. Thanks for always championing me along my journey. You both mean so much to me, even though it isn't always said.

Daniel and Patricia Doerr, aka Mom and Dad. Dad, thanks for giving me business and financial advice. Mom, thanks for humoring my big ideas and teaching me some of the awesome lessons woven throughout this book.

Don Fertman—Fellow music lover, friend, and University of New Haven alumnus, thank you for allowing me to include your inspiring story in my book. You are an inspiration.

Daniel Varela—Thank you for being on my journey, translating, and helping me locate my birth mother and siblings. Without you, the experience would not have been what it was. Your generosity inspires me to pay it forward.

EvaMarie Fox—You have been my cheerleader and confidant since 2005. I am forever grateful we have been a part of each other's journey for so long.

Gia Vacca—Even though you are no longer physically here, I still feel your presence in my heart and work. Thanks for inspiring me to think big and never give up.

Joe Franco—We met at the University of New Haven, and I am so glad we kept in touch. When you became my mentor in 2018, it was truly a game-changer. You helped guide me through professional limbo and believed I could be my own boss.

Maria Edelmira Ocampo Ayala, aka my biological mom—Meeting you was a dream come true. Thank you for giving me the gift of life.

Marco Matute—Thank you for being my cheerleader in my entrepreneurial journey and for believing in my businesses and this book.

Nick and Shannon Seyda—Your story and positive mindset are the perfect addition to this book. Thank you for opening your life to me.

Patrick Snow—You encouraged me to table my other book and write something far more important and inspiring—my story. I knew I had "a story," but I thought it was no big deal. You made me see there is a need for my words and through them I can help bring joy to others.

Peter and my boys Luca and Enzo—Thank you for being my rocks and the reason for my success. Thank you for giving me the time and support to create this book.

Sonny Vaccaro—Thank you for allowing me to interview you for the final chapter. Your wisdom and contribution to the sports world are hall-of-fame worthy.

Steve, Maureen, Meg, and Sara, my in-laws—Thank you for being a part of the book writing process by printing out the manuscript for me when my printer was busted and spending time with the boys so I had some time to write.

AMANDA MOTTOLA

CONTENTS

INTRODUCTION
IMMIGRATING TO OPPORTUNITY

"There are no extra pieces in the universe. Everyone is here because he or she has a place to fill, and every piece must fit itself into the big jigsaw puzzle."

— Deepak Chopra

At first glance, you may think I am an average American woman with dark hair and brown eyes, but if you break through the surface, a much bigger and more complex story is waiting to be told. My life started in the heart of South America on January 17, 1989, just before a military coup overturned a thirty-five-year "El Stronato" military dictatorship in Paraguay. My birth mother was only fifteen when I was taken from her and put into foster care. On February 3, 1989, Alfredo Stroessner Matiauda was exiled to Brazil and granted political asylum. In December of 1989, I immigrated to the United States when I was eleven months old, and my adoption has been a journey full of blessings, lessons, and opportunities.

A big part of my success is due to my childhood, upbringing, and values. I was adopted into a strong, loving, moral, and supportive family. However, growing up and figuring out my purpose and where I fit in was an emotional struggle. Physically, I was living the dream, but mentally, I was in a battle against my own mind. For the last three decades, I have felt suffocated, unacknowledged, lonely, and undervalued, but I have also felt liberated, empowered, uplifted, and respected. The mind is a wonderful and powerful thing, but it can also be tricky. Over the years, it has led me astray. However, through a positive mind-set, and despite getting deterred at times, I have kept returning to my destined path. When I had children, my life changed in a profound way; I actively committed to creating a better life for them, which, in turn, committed me to a better life for myself because if I don't take care of me, then I can't successfully care for them or inspire anyone else.

Are you feeling unfulfilled in your career or relationships or just stuck in your own skin? Are you constrained by living paycheck to paycheck? Do you find yourself wishing away time so you can get to that vacation or next thing that gives you temporary happiness? Do you take time for granted rather than focusing on what is most important to you?

It is okay if you answered yes to any of these questions. Just remember that life will always whiz by with the tick-tock of the clock. You will blink, and a year will have passed. If you are living, you are a step closer to approaching another new chapter and milestone. Life is full of ups and downs, and that is the way life is supposed to be, and with the right tools and headspace, you can be your best self and live a life worth living. I have found a way to live my best life by balancing happiness with life's curveballs. It isn't easy, and it is most definitely an ongoing journey. However, I am here to tell you that you can start from being no one and elevate yourself by doing whatever lights you up inside.

The negative feelings lurking in your mind will make it hard for you some days, perhaps to the point where you may even want to throw in the towel. This book will give you a backstage pass to my life and some real-life unfiltered stories of other amazing people. If you open your heart and mind and reflect on the words in this book, it should spark a fire within you to connect with others and achieve your wildest dreams. Some of the stories may remind you of past feelings or feelings you may be experiencing right now. Embrace the fact that we are not alone in this world. Take advantage of this digital age and the ease of connecting with and learning from each other. Regardless of your past, race, language, religion, gender, or experience, you can be your own leader, overcome your fears, and find success in your career, whatever that may look like.

Please take in all my words. The forthcoming stories are important inspirational lessons that can help you reinvent yourself 365 days of the year. I hope you will choose to actively commit to learning, listening, and evolving in your own personal journey wherever that may lead you. Learning is a lifelong journey, and only you can take that journey for yourself. I see you and I believe in you. Remember, there is a special gift within you—share it with the world. As scary as that may sound, all you need to do is start. There is no better time to start than today.

Together, word by word, through the next twenty chapters, we will learn, reflect, and bear it all together, and we will come out on the other side bigger and better. Are you ready to be your own leader, overcome your fears, and find success in your career? Believe it, overcome it, and do it with all your heart. Let's start right now!

Amanda Marie Mottola

AMANDA MOTTOLA

CHAPTER 1
OVERCOMING INSECURITIES

"Because one believes in oneself, one doesn't try to convince others. Because one is content with oneself, one doesn't need others' approval. Because one accepts oneself, the whole world accepts him or her."

— Lao Tzu

Being Adopted

You are walking along a path enjoying the scenic view when suddenly you turn the corner, look back, and realize the breadcrumbs have dissolved. You don't know where you are or how you got there. Then you peer up at the massive tree of life in front of you and notice a placard that says, "Family Tree." Other people are looking up at this tree and smiling, arms linked with their family members' as they softly discuss their lineage. Meanwhile, you look up and see nothing, and you have no one next to you to discuss it with. Your past and family tree have been erased. You are alone, confused, and lost.

Not knowing anyone who looks like you can be sad and lonely. That is basically the feeling you have when you are adopted.

Early childhood's innocence is wonderful. However, when the rose-colored glasses come off, everything around you may suddenly change. You find yourself asking questions about the past, family health, and life. Every thought, emotion, and experience is suddenly intensified. Things that never mattered when you were a little kid, like the clothes on your back, the color of your skin, and the thoughts and words you say and think, now carry more weight and can cause harm.

People can be so mean sometimes, and sometimes we can be our own biggest adversaries. The middle school and high school years can be brutal when it comes to self-confidence, decision making, and composure. These years for me were filled with poor choices, detachment, and confusion, with some peer pressure, reckless behavior, and an extreme desire to fit in and be "accepted," whatever that means, thrown in. This awkward stage is a normal rite of passage and hard enough in itself, but then add in the layer of being adopted and you will understand where I was coming from.

As I entered middle school, my awareness of being adopted and having immigrated to the United States grew like a Japanese Knotweed. I became more and more obsessed with my past, or lack thereof, and I began to feel like an alien. These preteen years are rough for a young adoptee, even suffocating at times. While everyone else was trying to figure out their identity in this beautiful little suburb, I was trying to figure out my identity in respect to my peers while also searching for closure and acceptance about my birth, adoption, and immigration.

I lived in beautiful Milford, Connecticut, a very nice, primarily white community. I could count the number of adopted kids and minorities in my school on my hands. Talk about feeling like an invasive species. Even though I was accepted, overall, I still couldn't shake the feeling of being different, and very few people truly understood what I was going through. Plus, it was a time when children's books didn't talk about adoption or race. Dora the Explorer didn't exist yet, and the closest Disney character I could relate to was Pocahontas. What I would have given for the movies *Coco* and *Encanto* to have existed then.

Growing up, all I had was a copy of my birth mother's identification, and I was fortunate to have contact with my foster family. My foster mother, Estela, would send birthday cards in Spanish almost every year when I was young along with a piece of ñandutí, the national artisan lace of Paraguay. Ñandutí is a Guarani word that means "spiderweb" because it is a beautiful spiderweb of lace. Guarani is Paraguay's national language, which is interesting because the majority of South American countries have Spanish as their first language.

Other than some ñandutí, a cedula (identification card), and letters from my foster family, the first eleven months of my life were a mystery. I dreaded my annual physical because it meant another year of not knowing my family's medical history and my mom writing in capital letters UNKNOWN on the paperwork. This always made me feel a little bit empty inside.

I also did not like when people would tiptoe around my adoption, apologize to me for it, tell me how lucky I am, or act like they understood what I was feeling because they didn't and never could.

Is there ever a right time to embark on a journey to your past? Will a specific rite of passage or event stir a eureka-like moment of clarity, shooting a beam down from the heavens, unveiling a neon sign: This Way to Connecting the Dots of Your Life! Wouldn't that be convenient? I hoped a sign would appear, but nothing happened.

I had existential questions about my past and future running rampant in my mind, but after a few more years, I stopped holding my breath and searching for a refuge to shelter me in the truth. I settled for being a typical, bratty, selfish, and sometimes rebellious teen who thought it was cool just to blend in and do teen things.

As an adult, I became more committed to finding answers and peace or at the very least acceptance of the past that I had no control over. I opened my heart to the possibility that I might never know the full truth or get answers to how I came to be, whether I was created out of love, or whether my biological mom ever thinks about me. After being open to all possibilities and letting Jesus take the wheel, divine intervention led me to a Facebook group for Paraguayan adoptees that changed my life. I discovered I was not alone in the United States—hundreds of other people had been adopted from Paraguay during the late '80s and early '90s. This group quickly became a safe haven of hope and a portal to share information, feelings, and questions. Shortly after joining this group, I met Daniel Varela, who would be paramount in my journey to the past.

Although nobody knows their final-destination or expiration date, most know their family's origin, what hospital they were born in, and under what circumstances. Growing up not knowing anything was frustrating. I prayed regularly for a chance to reunite with my birth parents and have the closure my heart craved.

Being adopted was a big cause of insecurity for me until 2014 when I embarked on a journey to South America to reconnect with my birth country and look for my biological family. It was a huge psychological risk, but if something is important enough, the exploration is worth the risk. Whether or not you are adopted, go into experiences with an open heart and mind because an experience void of expectation is an experience without disappointment—remember the outcome you desire is not guaranteed.

Being adopted isn't easy, and not everyone is adopted into better circumstances. The emotional ramifications and benefits vary from person to person. The following disorders have been found to affect some adoptees.

- **Oppositional Defiant Disorder (ODD)** is a behavioral disorder marked by defiant and disobedient behavior to authority. This disorder is likely to be caused by environmental and genetic factors.

- **Attention-Deficit/Hyperactivity Disorder (ADHD)** is a pattern of hyperactivity, impulsivity, and ongoing inattention that interferes with daily activities.

- **Conduct Disorder** is a behavior disorder that affects children with antisocial behaviors.

- **Major Depressive Disorder** is a mood disorder that can affect daily functioning due to sadness and loss of interest.

- **Separation Anxiety Disorder** can cause worry, a fear of being lost from friends and family, or fear of something bad happening if the persons suffering from it is not with a certain person.

There is nothing cookie-cutter about the adoption experience. Each adoptee copes differently and not everyone experiences the above disorders, but it is important to note that adoptees have an increased risk of abusing drugs and are four times more likely to attempt suicide than those who grow up with their biological families.

However, there are ways that you as an adoptive parent, sibling, or support person can be there for the adoptee(s) in your life. If you are adopted or know someone who is adopted, it is important to be aware of the resources and outlets available if help is needed. Don't be afraid to seek out a trusted friend or family member, therapist, counselor, or psychologist. If you or someone you know is experiencing suicidal thoughts, please immediately contact 1-800-273-8255 to reach the National Suicide Prevention Lifeline. For those outside of the United States, please go to www.findahelpline.com. You never know what emotional trauma someone is experiencing, so it is important to remember empathy and kindness because it can make a huge difference in someone's life.

Exercise

1. Grab your notebook. Imagine you knew you would wake up with amnesia tomorrow and might never regain your memory. Write down special dates and people you want to remember.

_____

_____

_____

_____

2. If you know someone who is adopted, have you ever asked them to tell you their story? If you found out today that you were adopted, how would you feel?

_____

_____

_____

_____

Leaving Communism

Robert Herjavec is an immigrant, entrepreneur, and author. He was born in Eastern Europe in 1962 and immigrated to Canada with his parents in 1970. His life looks quite exciting and happy now, but that wasn't always the case. His family escaped communism in the former Yugoslavia. For speaking out against the government, his dad was imprisoned, which wasn't uncommon in a communist regime. Fortunately, his father was able to escape and flee the country along with his wife and son. They fled in hopes of a better and safer future.

Herjavec arrived in Nova Scotia as a young boy and did his best to adjust to a new country and his poor economic status. To make ends meet, he waited tables, delivered papers, and then created a computer company from his basement. Fortunately, Herjavec didn't let financial or cultural differences deter him from creating a life for himself in North America. He knew he could honor the sacrifice his parents made by following the lessons and values they instilled in him, so he worked hard and dedicated himself to his entrepreneurial endeavors.

Today, Herjavec has become a highly successful and recognizable North American businessman and investor. He went on to build and sell several IT companies. In 2013, he created the Herjavec Group, a leading cyberse-curity firm specializing in security services, identity theft prevention, and compliance serving enterprises all over the world.

We feel insecurity when we feel different and try to fit in and be accepted. This can be caused by cultural differences like language, attire, manner-isms, and religion, but also by how the outside world views us physically or financially. Insecurity can be a roadblock to success and your dreams. Next time insecurity takes over, remember individuals like Robert have come out on top despite the odds. You can too. If you aren't proud of your past, use that energy to change your future. If you are proud of your past, use that energy to fuel your success!

Exercise

1. What would your first step be in learning about your lineage? Do you want to explore where the apple fell from?

    _____

    _____

    _____

    _____

2. Document as much as you can about your parents, their siblings, and your grandparents if you are fortunate enough to know them or have heard stories about them. The greatest asset when it comes to capturing the details of a family tree is your family. Don't wait until loss or tragedy to try to remember what they told you.

_____

_____

_____

_____

3. If you had to flee your country tomorrow and leave behind your belongings with the exception of one bag, what would you bring?

_____

_____

_____

_____

Being Different

Do you remember a time you felt uncomfortable in your own skin? Have you ever felt like an outcast? I will be the first to admit I am not immune to feelings of loneliness. Like most people, I have felt the pain of exclusion.

When I was small, my cousin, Aunt Barb and Aunt Sharon, Grandma, and I were sitting in my grandma's kitchen getting ready to have homemade pumpkin pie before we dived into a competitive Skip-Bo game. We were sitting at the table enjoying each other's company while the men sat around the television in the living room watching *Jeopardy*. My aunt commented on my cousin's complexion, hair color, eyes, and even her brittle nails. My aunt said my cousin "looked just like a Doerr."

Through this entire conversation, I sat there wishing I could just fade away. I felt almost naked because I shared no physical characteristics with anyone in the room. My other aunt must have sensed my discomfort, or just realized I was still sitting quietly in the room, and said, "Amanda, you have such pretty hair and nails." Although the comment was good-hearted and true, it added a little salt to a wound that never seemed to heal. I wondered what having a family that looks like me would be like. At least then I could avoid situations like this one that focused on me being physically different and out of place.

Strangers, friends, and even family have made all of us feel odd and left out at least once. Many situations foster this odd duck feeling. The exact situation doesn't matter. At some point, we have been excluded. Trust me; you aren't crazy for feeling out of place. Remember, though, that while it is an undesirable feeling, it doesn't have to define or derail you. You are entitled to feel sad, but you are also entitled to feel connected, like you are a part of something.

The next time you feel left out, take a step back and know that you are uniquely you and the gifts you bring to this world are valuable. Your gifts, talents, and presence are worth celebrating, so never let anyone tarnish your shine or diminish your value. Sometimes we concoct feelings in our head because our reality tells us we need to be perfect and always happy. No one is happy and perfect all the time.

I don't believe my relatives set out to make me feel left out or upset. If I had let my emotions take the backseat, I would have seen I was loved and looking different from my family didn't change that. On the other hand, in the case of cliques, bullies, etc., in most cases, you control whom you associate with or at least how you react. Try to surround yourself with people who like you for you and have respect for your feelings. If you are associating with people who don't make you better or lift you up, move on so you can thrive.

Feeling left out happens to everyone. You can redirect the negative energy and build a mental toughness by training your brain to overcome it. The more you practice redirecting and being tough, the easier it will be to recover from hurt. Being different isn't always a bad thing. I like being the only dark-haired and adopted person in my family. It makes me special and unique, and the older I get, the more I like standing out from the crowd. Life would be so boring if we were all the same. Don't be afraid to share your story because you never know who will connect with it.

Exercise

1. How do you find comfort in uncomfortable situations?

    _____

    _____

    _____

    _____

2. Ask your spouse, parent, or another person close to you if they have experienced being different. How did it affect them?

_____

_____

_____

Meeting an American

Have you ever wanted to live somewhere else? Do you ever stop to think about how lucky you are? Some people in the world are living on dirt floors, going to the bathroom in a hole, and existing in ways we might think only happen on television. The fast-paced, dog-eat-dog world we sometimes get caught up in makes it easy to lose sight of the blessings we have that others may only dream about.

I was meeting my friend Melissa Marcarelli in Middletown, Connecticut, for dinner. I was early, so I decided to take a walk and explore the downtown shops. I found a small bodega called EcuaExpress. I noticed some soccer items in the window, and *ecua* to me indicated the shop was His-panic-owned. I moseyed into the store and was greeted by a Hispanic man named Carlos. I said, "Hola," and proceeded to browse. The store wasn't very big and had various convenience store items. I grabbed a crisp, cold drink to support the business.

I asked Carlos if he were the owner, telling him I was adopted from Par-aguay. Then he told me his story, and boy was I happy I had pushed past superficial small talk with Carlos. I listened intently. I learned he had been smuggled into the United States over the border via a coyote (colloquial term for someone who smuggles immigrants across the Mexico-United States border). He explained that the journey took twenty-four days and he had traveled through seven different places, including San Jose and Cancun.

He spent five nights walking through the desert with hardly any food or water. This part of his journey was exhausting and terrifying. He said, "When you are scared for your life—I just can't explain the feeling—you don't need food or water; you just keep going and don't look back."

Carlos focused on his dream; in his mind, the destination of this scary journey, a life in the United States, made the opportunity worth the risk even if that meant dancing with death. The story was intense, but he explained he

desperately wanted to have a shot at the American Dream—a life he could be proud of that didn't exist for many in Central or South America. The United States was synonymous with opportunity if you put in the work. Carlos wants to be called an American, and in the next few years, he will achieve his citizenship. He said, "I have $10,000 in the bank to my name; I feel like an American. I own this business, and I work hard for what I have. This is the American Dream. I did it and others can too!" He no longer has the bodega, but he is planning to start a masonry business.

The American Dream is alive and well, and others can take advantage of the opportunity simply because they live in the United States. Many immigrants in this country value America and the privilege of living here more than some natural-born Americans. As Americans, we often feel entitled to what isn't guaranteed or necessary for survival. I am pleased I met Carlos and took the time to listen and learn from his story. Connecting with and learning from others is what life is all about. Don't miss out on the lessons right in front of you.

Exercise

1. What life essentials do you sometimes take for granted (e.g., water, health, etc.)?

   _____

   _____

   _____

2.   Next time you have time to kill, explore your local community, strike up a conversation with someone you don't know, and really listen and learn from their journey. Everyone has a story, and we always need to hear what they have to say.

Learning to Communicate

They said core classes would be easy-peasy. I believed I was enrolling in a simple communication course, an easy A with minimal effort. However, whoever "they" are obviously never had Professor Blader. As a junior, Communications 101 should have been a cakewalk for me. I took it toward the end of my college career so I could allocate more of my energy to an internship.

Class was good and easy. I enjoyed the content and homework. I always had an answer to the questions. It was like the honeymoon stage of a relationship at first, but once we got into the semester, the likelihood of me being called on was slim. I had a better chance of winning the Mega Millions. I would wave my hand in the air, and the professor would see me, look away, and call on someone who didn't even have their hand up. As a chronic teacher's pet, his behavior offended me, and I'm not easily offended. Whoever the professor called on couldn't have answered the question correctly if their life depended on it.

I can't totally blame my classmates for sleeping through an 8 a.m. class on a Friday. But I became frustrated that I wasn't being acknowledged. One day in class, Professor Blader talked about the final exam, which was a twenty-to-thirty-page writing assignment that would make up most of our grade. Initially, I was excited. I liked writing, and this meant I didn't have to prepare for another test. I almost never finished tests on time, so my anxiety with fifteen minutes left and several pages to go wouldn't be an issue. But then, he proceeded to tell us the topic.

"Class, I want you to interview your family members and learn about your family tree, where you come from, how you got here, etc."

Normally, this would have been a cool opportunity to learn and write. However, I was the elephant in the classroom—I was adopted. All those feelings of being different and alone that I had felt when I was in the room with my grandma, aunts, and cousin came flooding into my brain, and I immediately felt sick. I love my family, but doing research on their family tree reminded me of my lack of roots. I knew that doing this research would only make me sad and more aware that my history was a big question mark. The gaping blank that is my past was filled with unknown medical history and a biological mom who most likely gave me up for money. This fear left a huge void in my heart.

Two rows in front of me, my friend Alejandro raised his hand. He was a meaty, tall, Latino jock who didn't have a mean bone in his body. Alejandro said, "My family situation is a bit…um...can I interview my aunt? Well, she isn't exactly my aunt by blood, but she is my aunt." Professor Blader responded, "No, Alejandro, I am not talking about your brothers and sisters from the hood. I mean your actual family so you can learn about where you come from and explore your family tree." I was appalled that our professor would speak to him in that way.

Alejandro is Hispanic, so insinuating that his ethnic background meant he came from the hood was not cool. I scanned the classroom to see if anyone else was up in arms about this. I could tell Alejandro was a bit stunned, but no one else batted an eye. Everyone else seemed to be messing around on their cell phone, doodling, or in la-la land.

After that conversation, I thought better than to raise my hand and ask about my situation, so I decided to ask after class. I went up to Professor Blader's desk and said, "I am adopted and don't know my birth parents." He said, "Well, that is okay. I don't want you to interview your parents about their family here. Learn about your adoption and find your birth mother."

I immediately flushed because it was such a sensitive topic for me. In a perfect world, I would love to do that, but my birth mother was in Paraguay and most likely didn't want me, and who knew how much information I could uncover by the project's due date. With half of my grade riding on this, I had to try. I couldn't even muster up the courage to refute this assignment. I wasn't comfortable with it, and I didn't feel it was right for a professor to demand it.

What did I do? I complained to whoever would listen to me.

After a while, I decided to do the assignment. However, I would do it on my terms. I wasn't going to let locating my birth mother or this professor stand in my way of an A. I began by interviewing my mom and dad so I could learn about their family tree. Through the conversation, I was able to learn more about my adoption. I saw paperwork, read my mom's journal, and got an in-depth perspective on the past. It made me feel more connected to and appreciative of my story and adoptive family. It also ignited a desire to visit my birth country and get some closure. Through this process, I had an epiphany. I learned a big lesson in communication that couldn't be taught in books. I was able to get a third-person perspective of my relationships and interactions with my parents, myself, and others.

Professor Blader pushed the envelope by creating uncomfortable situations with the hopes that people would effectively communicate with each other. Looking back, I could have just stood up for myself and said, "Professor, I am not comfortable with this assignment and don't feel it is right of you to ask me to find my birth mother, which is a personal matter." This would have assuaged my anger and been effective communication. I also learned that sometimes, as humans, we get way too comfortable with the mundane and become fearful of the unknown.

We all have insecurities, things that scare us, but what if we threw those insecurities to the wind? If our first reaction is to go on the offensive and reject a new thought or idea because it makes us uncomfortable, maybe that is a big neon sign telling us to look deeper and see why we are acting from fear, step back, and open our minds to the opportunity awaiting us. Doing so may inspire personal growth and even send us on a personal mission to travel to two countries to find our birth family.

I went on to be fully transparent in my final paper. I allowed myself to freely share my experience and lessons learned. To this day, I keep in touch with Professor Blader, and I even wrote him a recommendation that helped him get an award.

Exercise

1. Have you ever stood up for someone or yourself at work or school, with family or with friends?

_____

_____

_____

_____

_____

2. Describe the teacher who was the biggest influence on you.

_____

_____

_____

_____

_____

Summary

I like to talk about what I call *immigrant chutzpah*. It is a combination of charisma, hustle, and perseverance, and it is alive and well in many immigrant entrepreneurs who leave controlling, poor, or disorganized governments and go to freer lands like the United States. Freedom of speech and other civil rights allow people living in the United States and other free countries to be what they want, live without fear of their homes being bombed, and achieve the dream of success and betterment by simply taking matters into their own hands. Overcoming insecurities about physical appearance, past circumstances, and the mental struggles that can be fear disguised as comfort are mandatory for improving life for immigrants and non-immigrants around the world.

You can only be as happy and successful as you are willing to be.

AMANDA MOTTOLA

CHAPTER 2
BEING A LEADER

"The greater danger for most of us lies not in
setting our aim too high and falling short, but in
setting our aim too low and achieving our mark."

— Michelangelo

In the last chapter, we talked about the many insecurities that can plague our minds. This chapter includes stories of people who are using their influence to be good leaders and inspire others. These individuals provide content and resources to the audiences they motivate, which creates a ripple effect of positivity and life inspiration even if the influence was unintentional. These game-changers are the world's past, present, and future influencers, parents, activists, athletes, and those doing big things for our world.

Paving the Way

Have you ever brought a child to work? It is a bit difficult to keep an eye on them, a job in itself, while getting your work done. However, this experience can be a tremendous learning opportunity.

When I was growing up, my dad was the senior vice president of sales and merchandising at Nine West in White Plains, New York. He traveled the world visiting malls to make sure people were doing their jobs and setting up displays properly. He went to Brazil, China, and Taiwan the most. It was hard not seeing him sometimes, but he helped provide for our family, and I got to learn about business.

In elementary school, I was fortunate to go to work with my dad once a year. I loved take-your-daughter-to-work day. My mom would put a beautiful dress on me, pack my bagged lunch, and send me waddling after my dad into his fancy office. He worked with mostly women, so they would gush over how cute I was. My dad would sometimes let me sit in his executive chair and answer a phone call as his pseudo-secretary. I also heard him talk to the clients. I always thought my dad and his executive job were cool.

Even though this special day only happened once a year, I got to spend time with my dad, learn about business, and even have a little fun. These experiences formed some lovely memories and inspired my career. I went on to write my college entrance essay about my dad and the take-your-daughter-to-work memories.

The road to your future can be paved at a young age. It might not start with a take-your-kid-to-work day. It could be teaching your child a sport, an instrument, or your favorite hobby—anything that inspires them to discover something they love. They might end up loving something so much it ends up inspiring their career path.

As mentors, parents, and friends, we need to lift each other up, be kind, and share what we know because we never know what young person we might be inspiring.

Exercise

1. What did you learn from your parents' careers?

   _____

   _____

   _____

   _____

2. What did you learn as a child that still gets you excited today?

   _____

   _____

   _____

   _____

Governing Effectively

An interesting book I've read is *If Mayors Ruled the World: Dysfunctional Nations, Rising Cities* by Benjamin Barber. It discusses a hyperlocal approach to government and how that might be the best solution for communities because history will ultimately repeat itself and national governance is doomed to fail.

Barber is a product of the Center on Philanthropy and Civil Society at City University of New York. He is a political theorist and author. In his book, he references several successful local governments and touches on the point that many presidents have political experience but very few have experience being mayor and running a small area, let alone a country. My own two cents are that maybe, just maybe, it would make sense to have a hyperlocal government or at the very least, require presidents to do a stint as mayor, then governor because a senator or representative who has never run a city really, in my mind, is not fit to run a country. We must pay our dues in so many professions by receiving certifications, continuing education credits, etc., so why shouldn't career politicians be held to the same standard?

I previously lived in Wallingford, Connecticut. Bill Dickinson has been the mayor there for thirty-six consecutive years. A big part of why Wallingford is such a nice, cost-effective, and safe place to live is the dedication and hard work of the town's fiscally conservative leadership.

Another example of a standout mayor is Frank Picozzi of Warwick, Rhode Island. He was a former contractor known for his festive holiday light displays who turned into an independent candidate for mayor in 2020 because he didn't like what was happening in the city. He beat the incumbent despite having zero political experience. Picozzi said, "I wasn't a politician... but, you know, I had the residents, and that meant a lot to me. I'm here because of them. They put their faith in me, and I'm gonna do the right thing. I'm gonna do the job as hard as I can. We're gonna make things better."

Mayors tend to be pragmatic and take a hands-on approach to solving the issues laid before them. They have a vested interest in their town's success because they live there with their family and see the residents out and about. Mayors can fix things and listen to their constituents at town hall meetings. Bill Dickinson and Frank Picozzi have done just that and been consistent while showing they understand the infrastructure and proving they genuinely care about the community at large.

If mayors like Dickinson ruled the world, things would be a lot more organized, taxes would be lower, electricity costs would be low, and communities would be in a better, safer position than they were yesterday. Although the taxes in Warwick are comparably high, Picozzi has done a great job in bringing the community together and adding a mom-and-pop sort of feel to local politics, which makes me feel more at home. Often, party labels, red tape, power trips, and procedures are way too convoluted and get in the way of a government's ability to thrive. Now is the time for us all to take a more hands-on approach to how our local communities function because high-profile, polarizing elections don't matter as much to us as local elections and decisions do.

Exercise

1. What would you do differently in your community if you were mayor?

_____

_____

_____

_____

_____

2. What political position would you run for?

_____

_____

_____

_____

Assuming the Role

If we all have purpose and a mission, we all have a role to play in the world. It isn't always glamorous. But whether it is being a rockstar stay-at-home mom, a performer in *Cirque du Soleil*, or a postal worker delivering bills, we all stand for something and have a purpose. This purpose is not only about our lives but the lives of others, even if it is as simple as brightening someone's day by delivering a Christmas card or as complicated as representing a client in a complex custody battle.

Matthew McConaughey is a great actor and businessperson who was born and raised in Texas. His most recent endeavor was publishing the book *Greenlights*. In my mind, it highlights how and why he is a great human, role model, and Renaissance man. I know if he ran for governor of the Lone Star State, I might just consider getting a pair of cowboy boots and a ten-gallon hat and moving to the state where everything is allegedly bigger.

In *Greenlights*, McConaughey takes his fans and admirers into the crevices of some of his biggest moments and reveals all—good, bad, and everything in between. One night when he was in college, he was waiting to go to a party and stumbled upon a book at his friend's dorm that changed his life. It was *The Greatest Salesman in the World* by Og Mandino. The book caught his eye for some reason. He read it from cover to cover. The lessons he learned paired with the values instilled by his parents, like saying "I can't" being worse than a swear word and his father telling him, "Don't half ass it," have always been in the back of his mind. Even after his father passed away, these lessons remained as a foundation for his body, mind, and soul, fueling his trek toward ever-evolving purpose and setting him up for success despite life's not-so-stellar moments.

Understanding and owning your role in whatever you do is important. It might not be the perfect role or your forever role, but life is a journey, not a destination, and you shouldn't stop moving forward and growing until you are dust. While you have air in your lungs, be open to each and every opportunity life throws at you, and most importantly, don't slow down at the greenlights.

Exercise

1. If you wrote a book, what would it be about?

   _____

   _____

   _____

   _____

2. What book has most inspired you?

_____

_____

_____

_____

3. If you could pick who played you in a movie, who would it be and why?

_____

_____

_____

_____

Breaking the Cycle

Have you directly felt or seen how important nonprofits can be to the people they serve?

At the University of New Haven, I took Dale Finn's business and ethics course. It was a valuable class, and I really enjoyed it. The content was easy to digest, and the professor's approach included an out-of-the-box, interactive activity. Our assignment was to break into five small groups, have each member nominate a nonprofit that meant something to them, and then, as a group, select one of the nonprofits to receive a donation. The next step was presenting each team's top nonprofit to the class, and then the entire class would vote for one nonprofit to receive the donation. Professor Finn told us she would make the donation in the name of our class, which was an amazingly kind gesture.

I archived this exercise in my brain as something I would do later when I am an adjunct professor.

One of my classmates got up and began talking about his childhood. His dad left, leaving his mom as a single parent trying to do what was best for him. She enrolled him in a local Boys and Girls Club in New York. He talked about how the programs supported him. Some of his best memories were from participating in activities through their programs. He said it kept him positive and off the street. His mentor became like a father to him and was a big part of why he was standing before us that day. He most likely wouldn't have even made it into college if it weren't for his mentor and the positive influence of the organization.

Wiping tears from my eyes, I saw the raw emotion of the journey this young man had taken to get to where he was, and it moved me beyond words. Although I didn't know him well, I was and still am so proud of him. I am blessed to have met this classmate on my journey because he opened my eyes to a reality beyond my own. I am grateful he escaped from what could have been a cycle of poverty, a cycle that becomes a purgatory for so many minorities.

This college course and crossing paths with this young man inspired me to step outside my own life and consider volunteering again. In high school, I had volunteered 400 hours of my time to the service of others. From running the children's choir at my Lutheran church to mentoring other students and making sandwiches for the homeless, if an opportunity came up to volunteer, I was all about it. I realized I had become so absorbed in college activities, studies, and internships that I had stopped volunteering. Sometimes it takes another person's story to remind us of what is truly important. A year after meeting this young man at the University of New Haven, I was inspired to mentor in the Big Brothers Big Sisters program. I mentored an eighth grader from Bridgeport, Connecticut, for a year. It was a great experience, and I hope my companionship made her journey a little better.

Lives are changed every day through the nonprofits we know and love. We never know where someone's path started, so help them set their bar higher and be supportive of their dreams and goals. If we can work together as a society to walk a mile in each other's shoes, be more patient with each other, act as a conduit for others' success, and help them overcome adversity through positive acts, we can help break the cycles that hold so many of us back. We should set the bar high not only for ourselves but each other.

Exercise

1. When was the last time you dedicated time to mentoring someone else?

_____

_____

_____

_____

2. What makes a good leader? In what ways are you a good leader?

_____

_____

_____

_____

Summary

True leaders don't run away from problems. They don't take advantage of others, and they understand that supporting the success and dreams of others will bring about collective joy and success. You will have many opportunities to look the other way, take advantage of a situation, or focus on your own agenda. However, if you stay focused on the bigger picture, keep working collaboratively through challenges, and remain courageous and honest, you will reap great rewards and earn respect as a leader.

CHAPTER 3
LIVING ON PURPOSE

"Life is not easy for any of us. But what of that? We must have perseverance, and above all, confidence in ourselves. We must believe that we are gifted for something, and that this thing, at whatever cost, must be attained."

— Marie Curie

In the last chapter, you learned about setting the bar high. Now we will discuss something everyone should strive for—purposeful living. This is a key component of achieving success and happiness. Over the years, I have noticed whenever I feel disconnected from purposeful living and being aware of the needs of myself and others, my health and happiness go haywire, thus interfering with my success and productivity and halting my journey. When this happens and you feel disconnected, it is a big red flag that it is time to wind down, reflect, and recalibrate.

Signaling SOS

Have you ever babysat a toddler and a newborn at the same time while the toddler was sick? I wouldn't wish it upon my greatest enemy. Daycare is a blessing and a curse for a parent because it requires a lot of prep. Not to mention all the illnesses that accompany daycare are enough to make a parent's head spin and immune system shutter.

When my little social butterfly Luca began his school journey for the first time, I was filled with mixed emotions. I was excited for him to make friends, learn new things, and get specialized attention that I couldn't always give him on the days I worked—it was going to be great! The school we selected had a great reputation and curriculum to help reinforce his colors, shapes, and socialization skills.

One Friday, I planned to spend the afternoon packing for our weekend getaway to New Hampshire. Instead, the day became a living hell that nearly broke me. After two short days in the petri dish we call daycare, Luca developed a cold that turned into an ear infection and then hand, foot, and mouth disease. This highly contagious virus consists of incredibly painful mouth and throat sores, and typically, only affects children. Prior to realizing Luca had hand, foot, and mouth disease, I was nursing and caring for our two-month-old Enzo while I attempted to nurture Luca through a grueling three hours of screaming, tantrums, and throwing a stuffed dinosaur at my head. At one point, both boys were crying and needing me, and that is when I hit my breaking point. So what did I do? I called in reinforcements. Three dots, three dashes, three dots, and just like that, I sent an SOS to my husband Pete because this ship was about to go down.

Once Pete got home, I was able to recover. He helped with the madness so I could escape and get a warm shower, which was like a little slice of paradise at the time.

The day was a struggle, and it was apparent I needed a break from the house. Since we had to cancel our weekend vacation, Pete recommended I get a pedicure and a massage the next day. Initially, I didn't want to spend the money or take the time away from being a mama bear, but the following day I escaped for a few hours to my happy place. I am glad my husband and child-wrangling teammate encouraged me to go because I didn't realize how much I needed a reset until I got one. I felt like a reborn woman—relaxed, calm, and collected.

When I thought about my kids not feeling great and how I had a thyroid flare up at the same time, I knew it was an awakening, a message telling me, as CEO of the household and my marketing agency, Otraway, I needed to make sure we were all working toward optimal health. Breathing in the fresh air outside the salon and basking in the sun, I was grateful for the day despite the chaos. I decided I would start walking or moving every day because I am blessed with two working legs and need to be better to my body for myself and my family. I also want to practice what I preach and encourage my kids to develop healthy habits; if I am not doing that, how can I expect them to take care of themselves or learn good habits?

We can get caught up in living on autopilot, engrossed in routine and materialistic things, causing us to take our family's health and normal daily life for granted. However, during these trying hours and days of poor health, we get the reality check we need to appreciate our health and routine.

Exercise

Challenge: Write down how you feel next time you fall ill and keep that text handy. On days when you feel heathy but defeated by work, home responsibilities, or the kids, look at this text and close your eyes. Remember how you felt when you were sick and know that this overwhelming moment is temporary.

Breathe deeply and strive to live purposefully as you open your eyes. This will act as a reminder that your health and routine is what powers your success. Take advantage of the good days because on some days you'll be sick and wishing you were going about your daily routine.

———————————————————————————

———————————————————————————

———————————————————————————

Inspiring FUBU

Did you know that many businesses start as a side hustle before they gain traction?

FUBU (for us by us), Daymond John's sportswear brand, is no different. FUBU was born while John was working at Red Lobster. He worked long shifts and then moonlighted as a want-to-be CEO. He didn't know what he was doing, but perseverance is a force to be reckoned with. He kept at it, learning, growing, and pushing for a future even he may not have realized was possible.

John's mom was his inspiration. She had a big can opener that said: Think big. She taught him it takes the same energy to think small as it does to think big. Despite being a single mother and woman of color without any connections, she kept moving forward and encouraging John to follow suit.

Daymond John grew up in Queens as a small fish in the pond, but he grew into a powerhouse shark. Kudos to his mother because her son went on to build a massive empire and is now the shark we know and love on *Shark Tank*. God bless strong mamas! Through John's upbringing and lessons learned, he has paved the way for minority entrepreneurs to show success can be attained if you persevere, live with purpose, and are dedicated to your passion. John is a goal-oriented individual with a formula for success. While attending his keynote and having the opportunity to meet and rub elbows with him in New York City, I heard all about this formula for success. Check it out:

- S—Set a goal.

- H—Do your Homework.

- A—Don't forget about *Amor*; those you love are your why.

- R—Remember you are the brand; learn to define yourself in three to five words. Life is a series of pitches, so don't get down when some don't go well.

- K—Keep swimming and don't stop; some people quit right before they make it.

Success and wealth don't happen overnight and certainly aren't limited to those born into someone else's prosperity. Everything worth fighting for requires sacrifice. Understanding your priorities and goals is important. Make sure you are being patient and kind with yourself because success takes time and energy—but you've got this.

Exercise

1. Apply the SHARK formula for success to one of your goals.

   _____

   _____

   _____

2. Who is in your circle of influence, and how do they inspire or support you?

_____

_____

_____

_____

Giving More Than You Take

Every January, New Haven becomes a hub of past, present, and future National Football League talent. I had the opportunity to attend the prestigious Walter Camp Weekend in New Haven in 2011. This weekend is a tribute to Walter Camp, the father of American football. It is filled with football recognitions, meet and greets, awards, and full access to amazing hall of famers and NFL-bound young athletes.

Through my Sports Chat Fanatic Blog, I was able to snag Walter Camp press credentials. As a nervous college kid, I spotted a very attractive and kind-looking woman named Maribel standing nearby. I explained to her why I was there, so she asked if I wanted to interview one of the men who was the first to dump Gatorade on a coach. I nodded and she proceeded to introduce me to a member of the 1980s Big Blue Wrecking Crew, Harry Carson, a former New York Giants player and her husband. When I asked Carson why he chose football, he said, "I used to play sandlot-style football when I was young." He didn't start playing football on a team until he was in high school, and he confessed his motive was "all about the girls." The sport proved to be more difficult than he anticipated, so he briefly quit, but he shortly returned and went on to create a football legacy that includes winning NFC linebacker of the year twice and being inducted into the pro-football hall of fame.

The "Man of the Year" award is given annually at this event. The award honors an individual who exhibits commitment to American heritage, leadership, success, public service, and integrity. That particular year, the award was given to Harry Carson, who is best known for his thirteen-year career with the New York Giants as a powerhouse linebacker.

On and off the field, Harry Carson is an amazing human dedicated to serving others, whether it is having a spectacular twenty-five tackles in a single Monday night game in Green Bay or motivating high school students, inmates, and corporate executives. Carson is committed to making a difference in the lives of others. He is a big proponent of supporting current and retired players and speaking out about safety improvements needed to prevent concussions. Carson himself suffers from chronic traumatic encephalopathy (CTE) and memory loss from all the hits he took in his career. He personally understands the negative effects repeated blows to the head, common in football, can have on the brain.

Although Carson appreciated the award, his mission is much bigger than just a trophy. He is a motivational speaker and understands that his platform gives him the opportunity to inspire and create long-term change. He uses his notoriety to spread awareness of not only athlete safety but other health-related concerns like prostate cancer among men, especially Asians, African Americans, and Latinos.

Even though fighting to improve NFL safety standards to help prevent head trauma initially ruffled feathers, strides are being made to protect players, in large part due to Carson's efforts and willingness to stand up for what he believes. Carson lives an inspiring, purposeful life and gives back more than he takes. After having the pleasure of knowing Carson and seeing firsthand his warm and enthusiastic personality, I know the "Man of the Year" award was given to the right guy!

Exercise

1. When was the last time you gave back to your community?

_____

_____

_____

2. Have you ever stood up against popular opinion? What was the result?

   _____

   _____

   _____

   _____

Dedicating Time to the Community

Do you strive to make a positive difference in your community? Dedicating time to our community betters our lives and the lives of others. Donating our time broadens our horizons, gives us perspective, introduces us to new experiences, and allows us to change what tomorrow looks like.

Upon my return from South America, I was convinced I wasn't doing enough good with my time or energy. After seeing impoverished people living what could have been my life, I was determined to do something not only honorable but that would pay forward my good fortune in my community. My colleague on the board of directors for Spanish Community of Wallingford (SCOW), Steve Knight suggested I run for a seat on the board of education in Wallingford. I mulled it over, did my due diligence research, and asked questions of the current board members so I would know what I was getting myself into. I decided I could handle the responsibility and time commitment, and that was the start of my first political campaign. I selected a campaign manager named Jeff Necio, appointed Peter (he was my boyfriend at the time) to be my treasurer, and hit the play button on this experience.

Some people think campaigning is like what you see on TV. That couldn't be further from the truth. It isn't glamorous or easy. It is a ton of work, especially with someone with zero political experience. I canvassed for hours upon hours, knocking on everyone's doors, introducing myself, and explaining why I was the woman for the job. I was the youngest and only Hispanic candidate to run, which both humbled and burdened me with feeling I had to prove myself. I started feeling like I wasn't going to be enough or I wouldn't be ready for a role like this.

I got an idea one day. Despite not being a morning person, I thought of standing on a corner during morning rush hour and waving my sign. I was a newbie in a town where name recognition and being part of the club were important for getting elected. I knew I had to go hard and escalate my campaign, so several mornings I got up early with my sign and walked down the street to the gas station by my apartment. I started waving at people during their morning commute. Realistically, I knew I couldn't knock on every door in town, so it was best to get them to remember my sign and name. Fortunately, my marketing degree served me well in situations like this. Guerilla marketing tactics, depending on the application, can have great success.

I ended up being elected, so my hard work paid off. It was a commitment of 350 hours over two years. It was a great experience, and I am glad I overcame my fears of rejection and ran a successful campaign, which allowed me to give back to my community.

Exercise

1. How many hours have you volunteered in your life?

    _____

    _____

    _____

    _____

2. Which causes, if any, are important enough for you to consider donating your time either as a board member or volunteer?

    _____

    _____

    _____

    _____

Summary

Living with purpose can be frustrating if you are searching in the wrong places. You must be willing to look within and dig deep to identify your calling. No one will be able to give you the keys to help you unleash your passion. But once you find it, you will have to commit to aligning all areas of your life to following your pursuit. It won't happen overnight, and it won't always be easy, but with the right mindset, a little motivation, and trust in yourself, you will be successful.

CHAPTER 4
LIVING IS AN ART

"The question is not what you look at, but what you see."

— Henry David Thoreau

In the last chapter, we talked about living with purpose. Now we will learn about how art and life are intertwined. Life holds so much beauty and opportunity to create amazing things. Often people forget to stop and smell the roses. They also don't appreciate the things that may look like a chaotic mess but are truly a work of art waiting to be crafted into a masterpiece.

Turning Trash Into Treasure

Have you ever heard of musical instruments made from landfill trash? The Recycled Orchestra of Cateura is a group of Paraguayan children who have done just that. They have toured the globe and performed for Pope Francis and various political figures while playing Mozart, traditional Paraguayan folk music, and some more contemporary songs. Their instruments sound beautiful despite being made from scrap materials collected from the Asunción Cateura landfill. This orchestra was founded fifteen years ago by Favio Chavez, who wanted to teach the children music.

The poor families in this area scavenge through the three million pounds of waste that is dumped into the Cateura landfill daily. They resell things they find, which helps them survive to see another day.

When it rains, the landfill floods and the community is forced to live with the contaminated water. Living conditions are not ideal, but an unintentional result of recycling this waste and teaching kids to play is the money generated from the orchestra's international tours, which has helped pay for developing the infrastructure of this impoverished community. They have also used the money to build safer homes for several of the group's families.

In an interview with NPR, Chavez said, "To be a musician, you have to be responsible, persistent, tenacious, conscientious, and sensitive. Without these values, you can't be a musician. But music has such a great power that it can't be just of the musicians. Music can transform society."

One person's junk is another's treasure, so don't hang onto that which does not serve you or bring you joy. Maria Kondo is a famous Japanese organizer, author, and talk show host. She is also a big believer in getting rid of items that don't spark joy. I think we can all take some notes from Chavez and Kondo. Be open to opportunities to teach, even when the odds are stacked against you, and only keep things in your life that spark joy!

Exercise

1. If you could play any instrument, which would you choose?

_____

_____

_____

_____

2. Are you holding onto things that do not serve you? Can you repurpose them into something useful? If not, can you pull a Marie Kondo and pass them along?

_____

_____

_____

_____

Surviving the Crash

Have you ever been in a serious accident? It can happen to anyone at any time for any number of reasons.

I thought I was hot stuff going to senior prom as a sophomore. I wore a stunning, light blue, Cinderella-style dress from Dillard's. My date was Mike Borelli, a handsome and kind young man who treated me like a princess. He invited me, and I accepted. When he asked if I had a friend who would go with his friend Chris, I set him up with my friend Kate.

Mike's friend Chris took us to prom in a 1982 Buick Skylark. The car had either been previously owned by a drug dealer or a senior citizen. It was okay, but not something you want to show up to prom in. We teased Chris because we were attending an affluent prom where most kids would be arriving at the Omni in New Haven in stretch limos, hummers, and whatever else tickled their fancy, while we would be rolling up in a tank. After a few minutes of teasing, he gave us a humbling reality check, telling us he had inherited the car from his grandma when she passed away. Insert foot in mouth here.

The prom was great, and then we went back to Chris' house and chilled in his basement for an hour or two until it was close to my curfew. It was a bit of a spooky evening—dark with some clouds, a full moon, and a Halloween-like fog. It sent chills down my spine. I even stalled for a few minutes before we got into the car to go home because something felt off. As we drove, we saw no other cars on the road. We got stuck at a traffic light and contemplated going on red since it was getting close to my curfew, but I said to wait. Even though my brother is a cop in Milford, I didn't want to take advantage of it. The light turned green, and we turned left and drove around the bend. Before we could get a few feet down the road, I looked up and saw a bright light speeding toward us. I heard the scream come out of my own throat, but it sounded distant.

I remember the impact like it was yesterday. It was swift, sudden, and devastating. The metal twisting and crunching sounded like a soda can, except this wasn't an easily smashed aluminum can but a 1982 Buick Skylark with a thick exterior. Then everything went black.

When I came to, I called my mom on my cell phone. I explained in the calmest tone ever that we had been in a car accident, and I was scared. I asked her to come get me.

When I hung up, I took stock of the damage. I had slammed my head against the side window and felt shooting pain in my face. I looked down at my feet and saw my flipflops were gone—somehow, they had flown out the window and across the road.

I checked on my friends. Kate had shattered the windshield with her head and was bleeding. Mike had most likely broken his ankle. Chris looked shocked and suffered some burns and back pain from his seatbelt.

I got out of the car shakily and assessed the situation. I walked in the road barefoot and stunned at the wreckage. I ran over to the car that had hit us. The man behind the wheel smelled of booze and was unconscious. I simultaneously called 9-1-1 and reported the accident. I looked up and saw a woman driving by at a snail's pace, rubber-necking hard. I ran to her car and waved so she would roll down the window. She proceeded to roll by and stare at me. I was a terrified fifteen-year-old and was rather upset that she didn't even roll down her window to see if we were okay. Within minutes, multiple police officers were there.

I was grateful we were all still alive.

I sat on the curb stunned and silent. I had no words for what had happened, and every bit of me felt numb. The world around me felt surreal and dreamlike. I looked down at my shaking hands and overheard the firefighters nearby. I don't think they realized I was listening as they talked about the accident. They said we were lucky. If we'd been in any other car, we would probably be dead.

My eyes welled up with tears. We had cheated death, and I am pretty sure it was due to our guardian angels' protection. Chris had inherited that car from his grandma for a reason. She had her eye on us that evening—it wasn't our time to go.

Did you know that, according to the National Highway Traffic Safety Administration, every two minutes someone is injured in a drunk-driving crash? Statistics like this are sobering, especially since it forces me to acknowledge that we could have been killed. Anyone can be hit by a drunk driver at any time on the road. It also is a reminder that if you are consuming alcoholic beverages, you have a duty to your fellow community members to be responsible and not drink and drive.

I remember looking back at the pile of mangled metal, shattered glass, and debris and seeing the accident through a different lens. The glass all over the ground shimmered vibrantly as the streetlights shined down, making the accident scene look like an abstract piece of modern art. Except it wasn't; it was a sign from above that nothing we have is forever and life is precious. I knew then that I had more work to do on Earth. The streetlights shined down on my friends and me to spotlight how lucky we were to see another day. Even the messiest and scariest accidents can lead to appreciating the fleeting beauty of life. Now it is time to live.

Exercise

1. How would you live differently if you knew you would die tomorrow?

_____

_____

_____

_____

2. If you passed a tragic scene or saw someone who was hurt, how would you respond?

_____

_____

_____

_____

Painting People

Creativity has always been an important factor for me when choosing which job to take. That is a big reason why Otraway is a creative marketing agency with the best clients. Recently, I had experience with an organization that prides itself on making it possible for woman to have beautiful ink on their skin post-breast cancer to cover their scars. Boobification Healing with Ink became a client of mine in 2021. We collaborated on creating some beautiful calendars to sell for their annual fundraiser.

I had never heard of tattooing breast cancer scars before and thought it was a unique and beautiful gift to aid in someone's healing journey. Trisha

Parenteau, the president of Boobification, explained that breast cancer survivors must navigate a "new normal" not only physically but mentally, and that the scars can be a daily reminder of a bad time.

Getting inked on the whole breast area isn't cheap, but sometimes a nipple tattoo for breast cancer survivors just doesn't look right. After her surgery, one of Trisha's friends threw her a fundraiser, raising enough money to get her left breast covered. Trisha was awed by the beauty of the art, and it brought her great joy and hope for what the future might hold. The tattoo artist found a way to turn her scars and hardship into a canvas for some amazing art.

Trisha's tattoo brought some much-needed control to a winding and uncontrollable journey, and she knew she had to pass this gift forward to help others on their breast cancer survival journeys.

Boobification Healing with Ink's mission is to help breast cancer survivors cover their scars and heal their minds through the art of tattoo. They partner with two amazing tattoo artists who have training in covering scars and have worked with countless survivors.

Many organizations out there incorporate art, creativity, and beauty in areas that might not otherwise seem glamorous or fancy. What can you do to bring some color and beauty to your life and the lives of those around you?

Exercise

1. What is the significance of your tattoo(s)? If you don't have a tattoo,

where would you get a tattoo and what would it be?

_____

_____

_____

_____

2. What can you do today to show someone in your community who is struggling that you care? Example: I like buying a stranger coffee, bringing a police officer a hot cup of cocoa when they are working out in the cold, or paying for the groceries of the elderly person behind me.

_____

_____

_____

_____

Experiencing a Love for Art

I always loved the idea of being an artist. I even went as far as investing in some beautiful oil paints, watercolors, clay, yarn, etc. I wanted to be the next Monet, but putting a paintbrush to canvas looks way easier than it is.

While exploring Rome on my and Peter's honeymoon, I spotted a small traveling Da Vinci exhibit down a side street and convinced him to go in with me. I am pretty sure you are familiar with Leonardo's most popular works like the *Mona Lisa* and the *Last Supper*. He truly was a Renaissance man. He is best known as an Italian painter and sculptor who also dabbled in science. I had the privilege of seeing some of his concepts and replicas of his works in the flesh that day, and I learned so much more than I already knew about him. He was centuries ahead of his time when it came to his mind and forward-thinking inventions. I highly recommend looking up his self-propelled cart, fighting vehicle, and machine gun. You won't be disappointed, and hopefully, it will tell you no invention or dream is too crazy. You have nothing to lose by trying to create something.

At different points in my life, I have introduced elements of creativity and used art as a form of self-expression. When I was in third grade, I had taken an interest in a keyboard while at my babysitter's house. I convinced my parents I should take lessons, and I still play to this day. During this time, I also began crafting fictional stories to impress a boy named Kyle Cole, my elementary school crush. I would write story after story about time travel, vampire bunnies, happily-ever-afters, and anything under the sun. Unfortunately, my love was unrequited, and these story gifts I routinely wrote for my crush ended up in the trash, but I didn't give up. I simply shook my head and told myself it just wasn't the right story to win him over. Even though Kyle and I never dated, we became friends. We went to senior prom together and had a blast.

In sixth grade, on a whim, I entered a poem about my adoption in a poetry contest and won. It was published in a poetry book. When I was in the seventh grade, 9/11 happened and inspired me to turn to writing songs. To this day, I have a database of hundreds of lyrics and poems, some of which are even copyrighted because I taught myself as a teen to copyright my work.

As high school graduation ticked closer, I practiced daily for college auditions so I could become a music therapist and use music to help heal people's souls, help those with dementia overcome memory loss, help children with various disorders to be calm and happy, and help bring this form of therapy to the East Coast. But not everything we think should happen is meant to be.

Although I am not a Da Vinci-like talent, I see great opportunity in the arts. The arts teach dedication, the power of practice, patience, and artistic exploration, which is good for the mind and soul. It is imperative we maintain these creative resources and outlets for people of all ages to explore so we may allow great minds like Da Vinci to roam freely. My hope is that school programs maintain the various art extracurriculars and programs for children all over the world and that the humdrum of busy adult life doesn't dull our creative instincts.

Exercise

1. How do you express yourself creatively—writing, painting, drawing, building, or some other activity?

   _____

   _____

   _____

   _____

2. What legacy are you painting for yourself? How will you be remembered when you are gone?

_____

_____

_____

_____

_____

Mastering Artisanship

Have you ever met a master artisan? Zach Kenney of ZK Painting is a Boston-based painter who has forever changed my view of conventional painting. He takes a job such as painting cabinets, a door, or a house as seriously as painting a beautiful masterpiece on a canvas fit for the Metropolitan Museum of Art.

ZK Painting is a forward-thinking and impressive company that only uses Fine Paints of Europe to give their clientele an out-of-this-world experience. It is evident they are committed to innovation. Their customer service and ability to exceed clients' expectations through their consistent and impressive attention to detail is amazing. They don't hire just anyone. They ensure that their employees have the skills or are willing to put in the time to achieve the skills needed not just to paint but to create works of art. Kenney values his employees and the companies they collaborate with on their jobs, from architects and designers to the crew with their paintbrushes in tow.

From an outsider's perspective, Kenney creates content on social media and does stunning paint jobs; his success look easy. However, it doesn't happen by magic. He attributes his business success to several key factors. From a young age, he learned to have a strong work ethic. Coming from a family of moderate means, he didn't have a safety net to fall back on, so failure was not an option. He had to find a way to thrive. He is an example of a lifelong learner, constantly reading books, asking questions, and working hard to invest in the best equipment, listen to the market, and adapt. He does not shy away from challenging projects. He will research and experiment with new techniques to find a way to make it happen. It also doesn't hurt that he is gifted with a tolerance for high risk and a lot of energy.

Kenney is also consistent with his Instagram and TikTok posts, always putting forth new and engaging content. His Instagram has more than 45,000 followers whom he obtained organically, and his Tiktok has 525,000 followers. His best social media advice is:

1. Post Consistently.

2. Be Authentic.

3. Be Where Your Audience is—Facebook, Instagram, Tik Tok, etc.

It's possible to be exemplary at whatever you end up doing. However, it takes some serious discipline, curiosity, and willingness to take risks to truly be great.

Now is the best time to begin painting your life's work.

Exercise

1. How can you level up the work you do to provide the best results?

_____

_____

_____

_____

Challenge: Observe your surroundings, take in the designs around you—from paint to the texture on the buildings and the construction of the roof or placement of the landscaping. If done correctly, a great deal of care goes into the services we pay for, so appreciate the talent and skill required to make our living spaces more beautiful. Jot down some things you may have not noticed before.

_____

_____

_____

_____

_____

_____

_____

Summary

Life can be a beautiful masterpiece if we let it, but we need patience to prepare the materials. Every great artist starts a project from scratch and may need to periodically tweak a stroke so it is just right. Our day, like art, is made up of many folds, chips, and layers of hard work, and diligence, allowing us to see someday the perfectly imperfect sculpture that is our life's work—the art we will pass on through our grandchildren. Living is an art and can be as beautiful as you desire to craft it, but only you can make the choice to actively live, smell the roses, see the beauty in each day, and strive to better yourself and the lives of your progeny.

CHAPTER 5
TAKING RISKS

"One day you'll wake up and there won't be any more time to do the things that you have always dreamed. Do them now."

— Paulo Coelho

In the last chapter, we talked about the art of living. Now let's look at some inspiring stories of individuals courageous enough to take risks. Some risks could potentially cause injury. Others can change the trajectory of our career or life, which can be extremely scary but also exciting if they work out. If we learn to take calculated risks, void of fear and apprehension, and adequately prepare ourselves before diving in, risks can reap big rewards, sometimes even be fun, and teach us something valuable.

Stepping Outside My Comfort Zone

Has your body ever been lit up by paint? I'm not talking about getting your face painted as child or dabbling in intimate body art as an adult. I'm talking about paintballs propelled by CO_2 (carbon dioxide).

I never imagined in college I'd turn in my cheerleading pom poms or pageant heels for a CO_2 canister, paintball gun, and mask. Nor did I think I'd be out on the paintball field shooting balls of paint with a bunch of guys and having paint whizzing around from all directions rapid-fire style, some aimed at my head, and getting welts the size of Texas. However, we surprise ourselves sometimes to keep our lives interesting.

During my junior year at the University of New Haven, my boyfriend and I joined the paintball club. We thought shooting each other would be good for our relationship, and it truly was—plus, it was a good workout. I enjoyed the sport so much I ran for vice president of the club. Every weekend, we played out a series of scenarios. One of the most intense was a reenactment of carrying supplies along the Ho Chi Minh Trail. One team had to transport supplies up the hill to the castle without being shot. The only catch was the person carrying the medical supplies couldn't carry a gun, so their team had to protect them or return to the beginning and risk turning themselves into a human-sized bruise. This style of play went on until the clock ran out—we had an hour, and whoever had control of the castle at that point won. It was an exhausting hour and really tested my stamina, but I felt so good at the end of the day and proud that I continued to play even when I wanted to give up.

Our paintball club played almost every Sunday at Yankee in Oxford, Connecticut. The September and October weather was ideal because you wouldn't get too sweaty and the foliage was gorgeous. The leaves would be an array of golden and fiery colors, and walking through the woods felt like being in the magical forest in the movie *The Bridge to Terabithia*. I also loved seeing the spray of colors throughout the course as people got lit up like Christmas trees with neon pink, blue, and various other colors. I preferred using pink paintballs because I loved seeing everyone covered in one of my favorite colors. I even contemplated partaking in some tournaments and playing semi-pro, but my wallet and studying for the LSAT convinced me otherwise.

I will not lie and say paintball is all fun and games or easy because it hurts to get shot, especially in certain areas. Plus, it really gets you breathing heavily and hyped up as you run through the woods without a clue where your opponents are hiding. I'm also highly competitive, so to get shot in an elimination game is brutal to my psyche.

I learned a lot from playing paintball. Protecting "your six" in team play, staying active, listening to the instructions for the scenarios, and cleaning and maintaining a paintball gun. The adrenaline rush when playing is unlike anything I have ever experienced. The agility and stealth you need to survive the various scenarios and courses is amazing.

Exercise

1. Describe an interest you had that everyone thought was out of character for you. Who was the biggest support of this new interest?

   _____

   _____

   _____

   _____

2. What is the best lesson you have taken away from a team activity?

_____

_____

_____

_____

Finding Ocampo

You are probably wondering what Ocampo is and why it needs to be found. Ocampo is my birth family's surname. Growing up, all I had was an eight-and-a-half by eleven piece of white paper with a faint copy of a young woman's cedula, which is like an identity or Social Security Card for Paraguayans. This fifteen-year-old was my birth mother, Maria Edelmira Ocampo Ayala, which is why the Ocampo name is near and dear to my heart.

When I was young, I often fantasized about my biological family and their story. Since I didn't know much beyond my birth mother's name, I made up stories to replace the mystery. Sometimes, my family was royalty; sometimes, they were jungle natives like you see in *National Geographic*; other times, they were rich and famous. I knew the void in my heart and my curiosity would someday send me looking for my biological family despite the possible pitfalls of doing so. Maybe they wouldn't love me, maybe they wanted nothing to do with me, or maybe they were dead. The thoughts scared me, but I couldn't shake the desire to know.

I was adopted in 1989, after Paraguay's dictator from 1954 to 1989 was overthrown and exiled. His removal left an opening for human trafficking and corruption. In the late '80s and early '90s, adoptions were popular, so baby stealing rings became rampant. Judges, lawyers, and other prominent figures accepted bribes, which resulted in falsified documents and illegal adoptions.

Regardless of what the journey had in store for me, I was determined to travel back to Asunción, the capital of Paraguay, where I was adopted from. Connecting with my heritage became very important to me as I got closer to wanting children of my own. I wanted to share that piece of me with my children. In 2014, I was ready to face the risk of being hurt and venture south of the equator. I was a broke college graduate, but I knew if I didn't commit to going then, I would continue to make excuses not to go. My fear, empty wallet, and comfortable four walls beckoned me to stop before I tried, but I was unstoppable.

I planned to leave in August of 2014, and I began telling people of my plans so I could hold myself accountable. I ended up funding my trip by collecting recyclables. I took them to the redemption centers for five cents a pop. My story gained media attention from the *Record Journal*, and before I knew it, people were rallying to help, dropping off recyclables by the truck full and cheering me on. Specifically, Hunter's Ambulance Services dropped off twenty-gallon garbage bags. My then-boyfriend Pete came close to killing me a few times after tripping over the giant garbage bags in our apartment but he respected my commitment.

A slew of people helped make my journey possible. Mr. Schaeffer of Meriden, Connecticut, reached out wanting to give me money since he didn't have bottles to give. He was in his eighties, and at first, I was totally against accepting his money because, as an adult, I wouldn't accept money from my grandparents. I would put it back in their wallets or buy something they needed. However, thinking about it and talking to people, I realized I would someday be old, and if I felt compelled to give and influence someone else's journey, my age should not matter. I would be incredibly hurt if someone rejected my kind gesture purely because I was old. I graciously accepted his money, having no idea we would become friends. After, I visited Mr. Schaeffer frequently—we watched football, I brought him meals on holidays, we exchanged gifts, and we talked about baseball—he was an avid Orioles fan. We have since lost touch and his number no longer works, but I am glad he was a part of my journey.

The news article also got the attention of the Paraguayan ambassador, Fernando Pfannl. He helped me acquire dual citizenship, connected us with the owner of the Gran Hotel Parana in Old Asunción, and picked us up from the airport when we arrived.

Booking the flight gave me such joy because I knew my dream of seeing where I came from was becoming a reality. We arrived in Asunción after some travel delays and missing luggage and embarked on a whirlwind five days. Daniel had already done some research and had a folder filled with documents, including those of potential aunts, uncles, and five siblings. Growing up, I had been a big fan of the Nancy Drew books, so this experience of following the clues Daniel had found was exciting. We ventured to a small glass shop, questioned a gentleman there, and asked if he knew Maria. He, in fact, did know my biological mom, but she had never told him she had a daughter from him. My search for Maria and meeting this man ended up helping my sister Raquel find her biological father. After running around Asuncion chasing some clues, Daniel had a clue that took us to the countryside. Another American adoptee whom he had helped find his family had a brother in Yaguarón, a potential spot where my birth mother may have lived at one point, so we chased that clue.

We arrived at my possible aunt's house in Yaguarón, and our guide and translator, Daniel Varela, told us to wait in the car while he went to tell her about me and ask if she wanted to meet me. Fortunately, she said yes, and we got out of the car. It felt like a different world. Horses, chickens, and other animals just roamed around on the dirt roads. My heart felt like it was going to leap out of my chest, and my hands were shaking uncontrollably. If this woman were family, she would be the first blood relation I had ever met.

When we pushed open the creaky gate, my eyes welled with tears. I knew right away she was my aunt. It was like I was looking into a mirror. Although she spoke only Guarani (Paraguay's national and Indigenous language), nothing was lost in the translation when we embraced and cried. Everyone in Paraguay speaks Guarani; only people who are more educated and have money tend to speak Spanish, English, or sometimes German.

She proceeded to walk us across the street so I could meet my grandfather. This was emotional overload and felt like a dream. He was spry for a grandfather, and I could see my Indigenous roots in his weathered face.

During lunch with my grandfather, my aunt walked over and motioned to her Nokia phone. Our translator, Daniel, said my birth mother was on the phone, and she wanted to meet me. She lived in Buenos Aires and would create a Facebook account so we could communicate and get to know each other. I was speechless. Not only was I able to meet some family, but they received me with open arms—and my birth mother wanted to know me.

I loved seeing my birth country. I felt a connection I cannot put into words—it felt like home. That trip really made me appreciate everything I have and how privileged I was to live in the United States.

Exercise

1. What is the biggest risk you have taken? How did it pan out?

   _____

   _____

   _____

   _____

2. Have you ever traveled to a country in South America or some other remote part of the world? If so, what was the experience like, and what did you learn from the people and the culture?

   _____

   _____

   _____

   _____

Turning Nothing Into Something

I reopened my marketing agency, Otraway, in 2020 after moving to Rhode Island. I did not have a professional network in my new state, and I had zero clients. This fresh start and clean slate was a bit unnerving, but it was also exhilarating to create something out of nothing. I knew that to be successful, I needed to put myself out there and let as many Rhode Island business owners as possible know I existed and could offer them valuable promotional product and apparel assistance in addition to strategic marketing plans. Immediately, I typed "networking events" into Google and came across a young professionals meeting at Harbor Lights in Warwick. I was nervous as hell because after being home with Luca for over a year and coming off a bad season of isolation, learning to live with a chronic illness, and spending 99 percent of my time home with a baby, I wasn't accustomed to being out in public, meeting strangers, and networking. I felt like the new kid in school trying to shake the fear of not fitting in or being the wallflower. I shook this unwarranted fear off and went to the event.

I ended up meeting some great people. One was Deivi, a local banker who was the sole reason I joined his bank. After I opened my business account, he mentioned I could set up a table in the breezeway to promote my company. I took advantage of the offer and set up my display, complete with a $150 promotional product gift card raffle for anyone who left their business card in the collection box.

When I returned to check on my display, hoping the box would be overflowing with business cards, I found only one business card—from a woman named Meg Mut, a local realtor and entrepreneur. I called her and told her she had won. She ended up using the winnings for a product to sell in her and her husband's new CBD store. She also invited me to a women's networking group where I met some amazing women, including Karen Dalton, the executive director of Dare to Dream Ranch, a 501(c)(3) providing equine therapy and various other activities to veterans with PTSD.

I immediately fell in love with Karen's mission because I have friends and family who are veterans. As we chatted, she mentioned something called

401Gives. We exchanged information, and since I planned to give time and money to the community through my Otraway profits, I made her that year's cause.

My business was just starting out. I had no revenue, so donating my time was the only option. My initial thought with my business was: Give, give, give. This giving mentality was spawned during my time in South America and by an inherent desire to help. However, if you give away all you have or more than you can afford to give, you won't be in business for long. My advice to any startup business is if you want to grow and hire a team, you need capital; you will have plenty of money to donate later if you plan accordingly.

A week later, I called United Way of Rhode Island to talk about the Day of Giving. I decided if they would have me, I would be an in-kind sponsor. I gave the equivalent of $500 in an in-kind donation. This landed me a spot on their website with companies like FM Global, National Grid, Cox, and more. It felt so good to see my logo somewhere public alongside those of reputable companies.

The 401Gives Day of Giving was a success. We raised more than $1 million despite the uncertainty of the pandemic. It was amazing to see locals show up for local nonprofits and give selflessly to help improve the community. More than 300 nonprofits participated. My in-kind donation went to a local nonprofit that turned into a $25,000 client.

I always encourage my clients to give back. It feels good and it will come back to you, sometimes in a big way, but if not, over the long run.

Exercise

1. What local nonprofit do you support? Why do you choose to support this cause?

    _____

    _____

    _____

    _____

2. What is the biggest financial risk you have taken?

    _____

    _____

    _____

    _____

Summary

Always living on the safe side without taking risks is not living at all. Being comfortable is nice, but think about all of the experiences, opportunities, and people you are missing out on by being overly cautious and hiding behind your walls. Taking risks takes courage. Taking calculated risks takes planning and thoughtful action. Some risks don't work out while others can lead to a whole new world just waiting for you to explore. It won't be easy. Results may take some time, and you may feel a whole lot of uncertainty. However, if you want big opportunities and to live with no regrets, put your limiting beliefs aside and go for it.

AMANDA MOTTOLA

CHAPTER 6
MENTORING MINDS

"The delicate balance of mentoring someone is not creating them in your own image, but giving them the opportunity to create themselves."

— Steven Spielberg

In the last chapter, we talked about taking risks. Next, we will get into the value of mentoring and being mentored. Our lives are influenced by others; sometimes, the influence is good; sometimes, it is bad, but what if we could strategically and selflessly mentor and be mentored in return?

Would you be willing to pass along your knowledge to someone who needs it, and are you willing to open your heart and mind to learn from someone?

Sharing Money Sense

Do you know the difference between the wealthy and the middle class? According to Robert Kiyosaki, the rich buy assets, while the middle class buy liabilities disguised as assets. Where do you fit in this mix, and is it where you want to be? Do you know what it takes to be rich? First, you need to determine what rich means to you and what amount of money you need to live comfortably because everyone is different.

Kiyosaki's approach to financial literacy makes complete sense. Why then are so many people living paycheck to paycheck or feeling a chokehold from debt and financial stress? Much of it is a poor relationship with money and a lack of financial savviness, coupled with some mental obstacles, specifically greed and fear. For me, impulse spending, getting sucked into credit card bliss, gift giving, and falling victim to good marketing and coupons were my downfall.

Letting greed or fear take the wheel of life is quite common human behavior. Greed leads to excessive purchasing, which is easy—just pick and click a button. Your credit card is already on file. The movie *The Joneses* (2009), in which stealth marketers infiltrate an affluent neighborhood to encourage rich people to spend more money, wasn't completely fictitious. We are living the Joneses' life every day, except our neighbors aren't Demi Moore and David Duchovny. Big tech, our own devices, and companies of all shapes and sizes bombard us with targeted ads, drip campaigns, and influencers flaunting whatever they are making money from. The consumer gets sucked into feeling they need unnecessary things, which leads to excess buying or even sometimes shopping out of boredom or addiction. For example, our society is hooked on all these free social platforms, which we think are used for innocent socialization, but over time, due to the addictive nature of the posts and sponsored targeting, our willpower to detach and not swipe becomes a figment of our imagination because we have become the product being manipulated.

While nursing my second son late one night, I found myself scouring the internet for baby products and other things I really didn't need. I was tempted and felt the fear of missing out (FOMO) when site pop-ups said things like "Sally Joe in TN just bought X" or when a product listing says "Low quantity" or "Limited edition" or my favorite mom influencer is posting with the best new teethers or convenience gadgets.

Remember, things are not usually fulfilling over time. The instantaneous rush of buying something "at a great price" can be great, but it is just a temporary fix and leads to further desire for the unnecessary.

Many also suffer from unfounded fears about money and employment. They worry about paying bills or getting fired when they are making plenty of money and have a steady job. These self-sabotaging money beliefs can block our true purpose and leave us feeling unfulfilled and stuck. We must manage the risks through financial savviness, discipline, and an intentional mindset rather than allow negative thoughts, impulses, or self-bullying to go on in our heads.

Manage the risks with grace and financial savviness. Don't give in to the pressure to keep up with the Joneses. Make your own plan, and don't worry about what kind of car your neighbor is driving.

By the same token, don't ignore financial problems. Such issues will not go away unless you make and follow a plan and maintain the right attitude.

Exercise

1. When was the last time you evaluated your finances? How did it make you feel?

_____

_____

_____

_____

2. What grade would you give your relationship with money (A, B, C, D, F)? Is there one step you can take today toward having a better relationship with money?

_____

_____

_____

_____

3. What can you do to build short- and long-term wealth?

_____

_____

_____

_____

Missing My Mentor

Moving to Rhode Island was filled with mixed emotions because I didn't want to leave our Connecticut home. In Rhode Island, I kept my business at the bare minimum so I could focus on raising our son and mentally survive the move while giving myself time to get acclimated to my new city and life.

In December, I found Gia-Marie Vacca's business card when I was cleaning my desk and decided to reach out to her to pick her brain about promotional products since my business was going in that direction. I had no idea she was from Rhode Island. I thought she had Connecticut roots because she had attended Sacred Heart University. However, to my surprise, she was from Cranston, next door to the city where I was living.

Gia was also actively involved in organizations supporting women in business. I had actually met her about a decade prior during an awesome event called Girl's Night Out at the Oakdale Theatre in Wallingford. I could tell then our paths would cross again, which happened on December 18, 2019, when she just happened to be in Rhode Island visiting her mom.

I was a little nervous reaching out to her out of the blue. But when I did, she said, "Congrats! Yes, I still have my own promo company. What are you doing?"

When I explained I also had a promo company, without hesitation, she replied, "We should meet for coffee or lunch. I would love to hear what you are doing and see if I can help in any way."

We met at the Greenwood Inn in Warwick and had a delicious lunch. During our meeting, I discovered her cousin had been a groomsman in our wedding. He was one of my husband's best friends. Talk about a small world.

Gia gave me some invaluable advice about not giving up and even tried poaching me from my own company. She said it was a standing offer in case I ever wanted to work with her. I was deeply flattered by this opportunity, but I explained I wanted to make it on my own first.

When I tell you Gia was amazing, I am not exaggerating. Her desire to help a pipsqueak like me was inspiring. Even though I was a new owner, and working in the same industry, she considered me her peer right off the bat. Her first inclination was to help others grow, succeed, and do things better than she had in the past. She was a prime example of a rockstar mentor with a mentality geared to sending the elevator down to pick up future generations.

Unfortunately, I didn't get a chance to truly thank Gia for the confidence she instilled in me, or the advice she shared, which has contributed to my success. We had trouble connecting in 2020 due to her heavy workload and staffing issues related to COVID-19. In mid-September, we had plans to talk, but we never got the chance. Out of the blue, she became ill in late September. On December 2, three months later, she succumbed to what ended up being cancer at forty-two-years young.

I will never forget this charismatic, brilliant, and lovely person. I still have her business cards, her number saved, and I talk out loud to her when I get in a rut or start feeling the imposter syndrome creeping in.

"Cancer sucks, and you were taken too soon, Gia. I will make you proud."

Exercise

1. What or who inspired you to enter your current career?

_____

_____

_____

_____

2. How would tomorrow be different if you made your passion a priority?

_____

_____

_____

_____

Mentoring Peace

Did you know it is possible to be mentored by someone you never met? Nelson Mandela was influenced by Gandhi, whose Satyagraha philosophy or *Truth Force* was a major driving force in Mandela's commitment to non-violence.

Mandela was a beloved Civil Rights leader who stood up against apartheid and served as president of South Africa from 1994 to 1999. He was a true statesperson, focused on representing the people and the common good.

Nelson Mandela passed away on December 5, 2013. It was a great loss to the world. He was a man on a lifelong mission to improve society and inspire the oppressed. He changed South Africa and its future, and his legacy will carry on. People like Mandela inspire faith in humanity.

Exercise

1. What have your mentor and/or mentee experiences been like?

     _____

     _____

     _____

     _____

2. Have you been influenced by a prominent public figure you have never met? What did they say or do that inspired you?

     _____

     _____

     _____

     _____

Educating All Ages

Have you ever met an educator or school administrator who was a cut above the rest?

Dr. Salvatore Menzo was definitely that guy for me! He started his career as an educator, then became the superintendent of the Wallingford School District for twelve years and created a name for himself not only in the district but in the state through various committees, awards, and innovations.

I had the pleasure of seeing Menzo at a town meeting when I was new to Wallingford. Then I got to work alongside him when I was elected to the Wallingford Board of Education. He implemented the Wallingford 100—the notion that *100 percent community involvement plus 100 percent student engagement equals 100 percent student success.*

Menzo is a strong advocate for furthering STEM programs in schools and believes community involvement is key to successful education. As the former superintendent in Wallingford, he put together a collaborative partnership with local manufacturers to craft programs that would intrigue students who weren't necessarily college bound. Teaching technical and soft skills alongside career-path lessons can be an integral part of future students' success. Menzo is truly a conduit for a better educational community and a driving force in inspiring youth.

Exercise

1. Is your work aligned with your passion?

   _____

   _____

   _____

   _____

2. What unique talent can you teach or share with others?

_____

_____

_____

_____

Summary

Mentoring is a powerful tool for both the mentee and the mentor. Mentors come in all shapes, sizes, and ages, and from all walks of life. Every successful person has been inspired, influenced, and/or mentored by another person, or in some cases, by a laundry list of people. Never underestimate the power of learning from others and simultaneously teaching others along the way. Learning is a lifelong journey, so if you have air in your lungs, your brain should be soaking up knowledge like a sponge. Don't forget to share your knowledge and mistakes with others and send the elevator down to the future.

CHAPTER 7
INSPIRING GREATNESS

"I became the kind of parent my mother was to me."

— Maya Angelou

In the last chapter, we talked about mentoring minds. Now we will reflect on moments that inspire greatness. Mothers are great at inspiring, and they typically seem to know what's best for us.

Remembering That Mother Knows What's Best For Us

Have you ever experienced the power of a mother's intuition and love? Award-winning musician Stevie Wonder knows what I mean when it comes to motherly love. He once said, "Mama was my greatest teacher, a teacher of compassion, love, and fearlessness. If love is sweet as a flower, then my mother is that sweet flower of love." My adoptive mom is a Spanish teacher, makes amazing stuffed bread, and is typically pretty understanding and flexible, except when it came to choosing my high school. Let's look back through a little first-person narrative:

The first day of high school is approaching and while most of my friends are beyond excited, I am not. As a teenage girl living in the suburbs who religiously checks out boys and desperately tries to stay on top of the latest clothing and make-up trends according to *Cosmo*, I am currently not a happy camper. My totalitarian parents have decided to enroll me at Lauralton Hall, a local Catholic all-girl school. Despite its prestige and high-quality education, I dread the sassy cliques, pearls, and lack of testosterone. Can you blame this thirteen-year-old, public-school, boy-obsessed chica for being a bit bitter that the next four years of what should be *American Pie* are going to be a Lifetime movie instead? Seriously, just kill me now!

I stare out my bedroom window, sobbing as my neighborhood crew walks through my yard on their way to Foran High School. They have some nerve flaunting their first day excitement in front of me. I fumble with the bottom of my way-too-long navy jumper (a tell-tale sign of being a freshman) as crocodile tears splatter my white blouse like Niagara Falls. My mom, who is also a Spanish teacher, aka my new, unwanted carpool buddy, yells for me to hurry up and get in the car so I don't make her late. I fix my knee-high stockings and put on my bitch face. Here goes nothing.

A few weeks into the academic year, carpooling is less desirable than I imagined, and the lack of originality of the navy jumper is getting old. Most mornings, I roll out of bed in my slept-in, wrinkled uniform, grab a cinnamon and brown sugar Pop-Tart, and argue with my mom because I tend to take my time getting ready, even though there are no boys to check me out. I find ample time on the short ride to school to complain about Lauralton since I have my mom's attention. She ignores

AMANDA MOTTOLA

me most of the time, which is frustrating, so I threaten to quit school or get out of the car and walk home. However, she always calls my bluff, knowing I am way too lazy and embarrassed to walk to school in my uniform. She repeatedly tells me it is an amazing school and not everyone who applied or took the test got in or could afford it. I just roll my eyes. Yeah, okay, Mom.

I quickly begin making friends and liking my highly competitive course load. One day, I receive a violation (and lunch detention) for refusing to bring my English book to class. I stop by Mrs. Dimassa's class to apologize for being difficult and make amends. English is one of my favorite courses, so I don't want to start off on the wrong foot with her. While milling around the classroom, I see a pretty older student anxiously and intently staring at her book. I begin chatting with her even though she is trying to concentrate. I am pretty sure she wants nothing to do with me, but I don't care. I am nosey and want to know who she is and what she is doing.

Spoiler alert—she became my best friend and the maid of honor in my wedding. Thank goodness, my mom raised me to be overly confident.

Have you ever looked back on a season in your life and realized mother/father knew best? If I only knew then that my time at LHA would be filled with the best educational experience, my best friend EvaMarie, and being matched with equally confident and competitive young women, I may have eased up on being so challenging to my parents. Here are a few of the extracurriculars I participated in and achievements I gained while at Lauralton.

Extracurriculars:

- President of Youth and Government
- Lieutenant Governor of the Youth & Government State Conference
- President of Amnesty International
- Member of the Environmental Club, Spanish Club, Humanities, Ballroom Dance Club
- Varsity Cheerleading Squad (as a first-year)
- Advanced Vocal Ensemble Member

Achievements:

- Won an award for volunteering 400 hours during my high school career
- Received the Daughters of the America Revolution Award
- Selected as the New Haven Youth of the Year (usually this goes to the valedictorian, which I wasn't)

It was a privilege to attend Lauralton—a privilege I took for granted until I got to college where I saw how overprepared I was compared to my peers. Some had never written a term paper. My rigorous college prep education had me writing term papers and presenting in my sleep. Deep down, my mom knew all along that Lauralton was the perfect place for me, and the experience there would ultimately allow me to flourish and become the woman, CEO, and mother I am today.

Exercise

1. Write about three events that were influenced by your mother or a motherly figure. If you are blessed to still have this motherly figure in your life, please give her a call, send a letter, or pop by to thank her. If she has passed away, write a letter expressing your gratitude.

    _____

    _____

    _____

    _____

    _____

    _____

Inspiring Like a Mother

Have you come across an amazingly successful mom? Ever wonder what led to her success? According to super-parent and author of _How to Raise Successful People: Simple Lessons for Radical Results_, Esther Wojcicki, it all stems from how they were raised.

Wojcicki is a role model for ultimate parental success. Not just one but all three of her daughters have excelled in their careers. Just look at what they have accomplished: Susan Wojcicki is CEO of YouTube, Janet Wojcicki is a professor of pediatrics, and Anne Wojcicki is the co-founder of 23andMe. Not too shabby—I would say her daughters have done quite well for themselves and that is in big part due to Wojcicki's parenting.

Wojcicki coined the acronym TRICK, which stands for:

1. **Trust:** Trust the process of the child's growth. Trust the child to make their own choices through the designated family routines with supplemental support. For example, help them set the table, pick out their own clothes, etc. Trusting the child's abilities empowers them and gives them confidence.

2. **Respect:** This is speaking to the child "as if they were adults from day one" instead of using baby talk. This is huge because children's minds are like sponges, so the more vocabulary they are exposed to, the more they will incorporate in their own speech.

3. **Independence:** Children should begin early. Fostering independence is imperative to empowering them to become independent adults. Esther uses the example of parents trying to help and/or protect their child by hovering. Unfortunately, the unintended consequence is creating a dependent child who then goes on to become a dependent adult.

4. **Collaboration:** The child should be included in the process of setting routines and making decisions so they have buy-in and respect for the routine.

5. **Kindness:** This should be given when people make mistakes. What is said is often forgotten. However, people will always remember how they are treated. None of us are perfect and we may at times fall short, but it is best not to harp on the negative or be unkind.

These tried-and-true methods can be quite effective in raising children who are motivated, respectful, and strong.

Exercise

1. List the ways you have inspired or taught someone younger than you (a child, brother, sister, friend, etc.).

    _____

    _____

    _____

    _____

2. How did it make you feel? Why did you do it?

    _____

    _____

    _____

    _____

Mothering Like Teresa

Who is the most famous selfless woman you can think of? Many people would say Mother Teresa because her positive influence and dedication to the less fortunate has had a ripple effect on humanity. She spread the concept of universal love and sacrifice for others, and she did so by example. She was so moved by the poor that she ventured outside of the convent walls to fulfill her calling and care for the poor in the slums of Kolkata. She opened a school for children, and soon volunteers flocked to assist, which allowed her mission to continue.

Mother Teresa was canonized nine years after her death. Obtaining saint status is not an easy process. It unfolds in three stages: evaluation, beatification, and canonization. It takes years for an individual's life to be reviewed and miracles confirmed.

Although most of us will not become saints, there are things we can do to make the world a better place and cause a ripple effect of goodness.

Any effort to show compassion, love, and selflessness is better than no effort. So give it a try and see how much it makes others smile. You never know whom you will inspire to pass it along!

Exercise

1. How will you actively incorporate service to others into your life?

_____

_____

_____

_____

_____

_____

2. Who can you treat with more compassion? Is it a boss, a parent, a client, a child? Go forth and channel your inner Mother Teresa.

_____

_____

_____

_____

_____

Loving Like a Mother

Close your eyes and imagine you are a parent waiting for news about your child. The doctor walks in and says, "Your child has a 3 percent chance of living." Thoughts race through your mind and the floor feels like it is dropping out from under you. You close your eyes and breathe deeply. What is within your control? Committing to a positive mindset in this moment may seem impossible, but it is necessary to set the course for the future, whatever that holds for your family.

Nick Seyda is a young man who has defied the odds, surprised doctors, and inspired people all over the world. The kicker is he is only seventeen and doing big things in the freestyle soccer world! Looking at him, you wouldn't know he is a miracle. He started life as a fragile preemie who wasn't expected to walk, talk, or breathe on his own. Nick's parents knew their only option from the beginning was to keep their hope alive by working through whatever the future had in store for their family. By the age of seven, Nick had powered through five major surgeries.

Nick became exceptionally talented at playing soccer and took training very seriously. He traveled for games and excelled until one day he began having some knee pain. The pain was from a rare disease called osteochondritis dissecans (OCD of the knee). Nick thought that with treatment he would be able to perform at the same high level within a year, but it was uncertain.

Then when Nick was twelve, he attended a NY Red Bull game. A freestyle soccer player passed him the ball. That moment changed his life, and he never stopped juggling the soccer ball after that.

The biggest lesson he learned from his mother was in October of 2013. He developed Chron's Disease and became very ill. He was feeling defeated, but his mom said if you can find that little bit of positivity in the future and hold on to it right now, it will get you through the bad times. From that moment on, he would look for signs and focus on future opportunities. He allowed his overwhelming sense of hope and optimism to push him forward.

Nick's mother Shannon is his biggest cheerleader. She studied developmental psychology at Columbia. She believes her career path was no coincidence because it helped her cope and lead her family through the challenge of having an underdeveloped child who needed special attention.

Shannon has some great advice for all parents: Life is never perfect so don't be afraid to ask questions and do your research to prepare the best you can. You are your child's best advocate, so encourage and commit to your child's success, whatever that may look like. You can achieve this by having faith and working together as a family to make the environment a positive and strong foundation.

Being loved and taught by a mother figure is a powerful force that can help a child overcome the biggest life hurdles.

Exercise

1. What has been the biggest setback in your life?

_____

_____

_____

_____

2. If you could be the world champion in something, what would it be?

_____

_____

_____

_____

Summary

Inspiring greatness takes kindness, respect, and time. It is not limited to mothers or fathers. Working with a team is the best way to raise successful and productive adults. Co-parenting is important to our society as a whole. I personally strive to maintain and nurture my marriage and my connection with my children. How will you inspire the future?

CHAPTER 8
OVERCOMING IGNORANCE

"It takes considerable knowledge just to realize the extent of your own ignorance."

— Thomas Sowell

In the last chapter, we talked about inspiring greatness. Now you will learn why ignorance is not bliss. The following stories are about times when hurt has been caused because of ignorant words and actions. It is also an opportunity to learn how unspoken and unaddressed ignorance can take away the opportunity to learn, connect, and grow.

Blessing Their Hearts

I am a Paraguayan American citizen, and I have been living in the United States for more than thirty years. I enjoy watching sports, especially football and futbol. There was no question that if the Paraguay national team came to play the USA in the Copa America, I would make an appearance. Philadelphia, Pennsylvania, wasn't exactly close, but it was close enough for a road trip.

Attending this Copa America game was a once-in-a-lifetime opportunity, and I'm happy my fiancé (now husband) supported my decision to go. He would have loved to go together, but he had a night planned in Hartford with his family who were visiting. Since you only live once, I had to go, so he encouraged me to have fun and bring some friends. I posted a message on Facebook explaining my need to go to Philly for the Copa America and asked who would be up for a road trip. My friends James and Melissa were game to go. It was super-short notice, so I admired their spontaneity. I booked an Airbnb for Saturday, June 11, and gassed up my car for the journey. It took about three-and-a-half hours and a little anxiety on my end driving in a new city, but we made it!

It was a great game, but Paraguay just could not get the ball in the net. However, red, white, and blue are my colors, and I have a lot of pride and love for both of my countries, so a US win was okay. When we exited the venue, we experienced a gorgeous sea of patriotic colors regardless of team affiliation; everyone was in red, white, and blue, so it was cool to see the unity. I loved having so many Paraguayans in one vicinity; it made me feel connected, even though we were all strangers.

I was on cloud nine taking in the experience until I heard someone yell at me "Paraguay Sucks. Woohoo! U-S-A! U-S-A!" as they pointed at my Paraguay jersey. Part of me winced. As a Pittsburgh Steelers' fan, I don't get offended when rivals make "Big Ben" jokes (mock Steelers' quarterback Ben Roethlisberger) or poke fun at a loss, but hearing someone dis my birth country was upsetting since being adopted really rocked my world growing up. Of course, I just shook my head, but internally, I was shouting right back. I have learned when to pick my battles, and that wasn't the place nor time, especially since in that moment, I was hangry.

My friends and I spent some time in Philly getting food and some cocktails, and while walking around, we saw many kindred soccer fans, or so I thought. A couple of men made comments to me like "Paraguay Sucks" or "Go Back to Your Country!" Well, sheesh! What if this is my country, and so what if I am first generation here? If only these individuals knew my story, they would maybe shut their mouths and have a little compassion for a young woman who had gone through some mental hurdles over her identity confusion in belonging to both countries. Why bother making comments like this, especially when you don't know a person's story and have not walked a mile in their shoes? However, as I will discuss later in Chapter 16, I know hurt people tend to hurt other people, so I blessed this man's heart and moved on.

Deciding to purchase Copa America tickets less than a week before the game and not knowing how or who I was going with was the most spontaneous thing I had done in a long time. As I have aged, I do spontaneous things less and less. I had literally hit "purchase" on Ticketmaster and decided I was going to Philly on Saturday. I had no plan for getting there or having accommodations. Even though there wasn't a lot of planning, it was such a comfortable experience. Airbnb is a godsend, and I have nothing but kudos to send its way for my stays in Argentina, Italy, and Philly.

If you feel as though your life is becoming or has become stagnant, then this challenge is calling out to you. Tomorrow, this weekend, or next week, do something spontaneous.

Exercise

1. If you could go anywhere this weekend, where would it be? What is stopping you?

   _____

   _____

   _____

   _____

2. Has anyone ever judged you based on your clothing? Have you ever passed judgment on someone else based on how they were dressed?

   _____

   _____

   _____

   _____

Appreciating What We Have

Upon my return from Argentina, I was really overwhelmed. It dawned on me what my living situation could have been in if I had not been adopted. Life would be a struggle, and I would not be running two businesses like I am here in the United States. This was a huge wake-up call for me. Prior to it, I'm ashamed to say, I had been oblivious to how I am quite privileged and have way more luxuries than a lot of other people. This newfound re-alization made me feel it was my duty to do something about the lack of opportunity that exists within the Latino community, whether it is systemic or self-inflicted based on societal norms and culture. This desire to represent *mi gente* (my people) and make life better for the sometimes-overlooked Latino population led me to run for a political position, mentor upcoming entrepreneurs and young people, and donate to organizations like Spanish Community of Wallingford. I began resenting my possessions. I wasn't planning to strip my life of everything and live like a monk. However, a woman does not need six different shampoos for one head of hair. I now consciously decide not to buy products just because I use them and they are on sale. I will not be a hoarder, nor will I any longer waste money on unnecessary purchases.

My mom is a big do-gooder and a big part of why I like helping others. While she was teaching at Lauralton, she led trips down to Central America and traveled to Africa. She helped to build several schools in Guatemala and had an opportunity to be immersed in the local culture. One day while touring a Guatemalan village, she saw what looked like some sort of oven in the ground. She asked the villager what it was. The woman said it was for pregnant women to crawl into and have their babies. My mom was a bit shocked it was not some sort of pizza-like oven. It was made of clay and far different from what women expect to have for childbirth in the United States, but this was the way of life for Guatemalan women.

While my mom was in Africa, she had the opportunity to meet individuals affected by AIDS, including young people who had stepped up to care for their siblings when their parents passed away and they became orphaned. This was a very humbling trip. My mom was able to see firsthand what life was like in Malawi, the fourth poorest country in the world. Upon her return from Africa, she had a new fridge delivered. Not until the delivery men left did she discover they had put the fridge door handle on the wrong side, despite her explicitly telling them how she wanted it. For the first few days, she reached for the wrong side to open the fridge, only to shake her head when she realized there was no handle there. We are creatures of habit, so when things deviate from what we know or expect, we get thrown off and frustrated. She then reminded herself that in Africa she had visited people who don't even have fridges. The fridge handle being on the wrong side was truly a First World problem and really shouldn't even be a concern.

Sometimes the privileges and advances experienced in more modern and First World countries are undervalued. It is important to remind ourselves that we are blessed to be living here because life is much harder where people don't have access to clean water, shelter, or food.

Exercise

1. I challenge you to find three possessions to get rid. For example, hats, shoes, purses, etc. Do you have a freecycle Facebook page in your community or a local church or homeless shelter you can donate to?

_____

_____

_____

_____

2. What in your daily routine is something that others around the world might not have?

_____

_____

_____

_____

Judging by the Cover

I am no stranger to being singled out or addressed in an inappropriate manner. I have been called a white Hispanic and other terms I do not wish to share. These judgments come from stereotypes of how people think a Hispanic person should or shouldn't act or look. It isn't right to judge based on preconceived notions.

When I was about fifteen, I had a summer job working at an Italian restaurant bussing tables. A woman said, "Honey, you speak English?" When I didn't respond fast enough, she proceeded to say, "I need a water," while slowly pronouncing each syllable and motioning at her empty water glass. The assumption that I didn't understand English probably stemmed from my very dark summer complexion and bussing tables instead of waiting on them.

Racism, xenophobia, stereotyping, homophobia, sexism, etc. all come from the same root cause—ignorance. When I look at my sons, they are innocent. However, they are constantly mirroring what we do, whether it is vocabulary, tone of voice, actions, etc. For example, when my toddler does something reckless or I get very frustrated with him, I say, "Never again." Now when he gets frustrated with me, he shakes his finger at me and says, "Mom, never again!" The apple doesn't fall far from the tree, and we can't expect our children to be much different than us or their surroundings. I believe people aren't born with hate in their heart or meanness in their bones. Biases and ignorance stem from our experiences and what we are taught and exposed to, but we have the power to think and act differently.

I don't personally blame the woman for assuming I only spoke Spanish. Part of me appreciates that she even acknowledged I was Hispanic because most people I grew up with thought of me as a white Hispanic, since I didn't speak fluent Spanish, have a *quinceañera*, or "act Hispanic." A *quinceañera* is a rite of passage for a fifteen-year-old Hispanic girl to celebrate her womanhood. It is typically at a venue with lots of guests and the honoree wears a fancy dress. Some *quinceañeras* are as extravagant as weddings. Part of me felt it was nice to be seen as a Hispanic woman. On the flip side, that woman's comment was a bit off-putting. Whether or not she meant it that way, she made an assumption and made me feel less than because of it.

The problems run deep. For example, one night Pete and I were watching a movie on Netflix when we paused it to take a snack break. In the background of the film, I noticed a Black man was being arrested by a white police officer who was holding him against the hood of a police car. The only reason I saw it was because we paused the movie. Casting by stereotype is common, and the background images are subliminal messages constantly put in front of us so that what they depict remains "normal and accepted."

How much of what we consume from various media outlets shapes our actions, thoughts, and decisions? Even though sometimes the stereotypes that exist come from some form of reality, can we detach from the generalizations and dive deeper into understanding each other and meeting one another where we were are rather than just rely on how the media tries to define us.

Exercise

1. Have you ever been judged based on how you look? How did you react? How would you react now?

_____

_____

_____

_____

2. What bias or preconceived judgment was passed down to you that you want to overcome?

_____

_____

_____

_____

Befriending a Stranger

Have you ever met a stranger and ended up having a really nice conversation? I was alone when I went to get fitted for my wedding dress in New Haven on Broad Street. Fortunately, I found a parking spot only a block away. When I left the bridal shop, I couldn't help but feel a little self-conscious carrying my designer duffel bag and a nice leather briefcase with my laptop. I was waiting for the pedestrian signal to change and thinking about going against the light—it was a small, quiet street with little to no traffic. Then I looked to my left and saw a forty-something Black man with a baseball cap, black tank top (aka, wife beater), and shorts. He had a cigarette in one hand and a bottle in a brown paper bag in the other.

The hairs on my arm immediately stood up. I had my keys in my right hand and held them like a weapon—discreetly, of course. I tried to stay calm when this gentleman entered my personal space and said, "Hello, do you have a light?" A million thoughts ran through my mind. He was too close for comfort, and I could smell the alcohol on his breath. I was on edge. But I remained calm. I would not let myself be controlled by stereotypes, even though in this moment they existed. After all, I am a minority, and I would not want someone to judge me based on what I look like, so I figured I owed him the same courtesy and respect I would expect to receive. In that moment, I chose not to see color, not fear the unknown, and give him a chance. "No, I don't. Sorry," I said.

The signal changed and we both walked across the street. As we walked, he said, "Can I help you with your bags?" I did look a little overburdened since I was rushing to get home before traffic started to get bad, so the question was innocent enough. I politely declined because part of me was scared he would run off with my brand-new bag, which was a wedding gift. To deflect my negative thought and my discomfort, I tried to be funny. I said, "I worked hard for these guns," and pointed to my arms, indicating why I didn't need help.

He laughed and said, "I am all about equal opportunity for men and women." I nodded, and he asked, "Do you make as much as your man?" I said, "Well, I do well for myself, but I don't make as much as he does because he is an engineer." He said, "That's great for him. What do you do?" I said, "I am in marketing and help promote liquor companies."

As soon as I said that, I felt a twinge of guilt because this gentleman before me was clearly hitting the bottle alone at two in the afternoon on a Thursday.

He replied, "You will do good and definitely be in business for a long time."

We exchanged names. His was Lorenzo. We continued walking until my car was about two yards away. I started walking toward it, and we continued chatting. He asked where I was from, and I said South America. We then started talking about politics. "You know how important politics are being a strong woman in today's society," he said. I told him I was a conservative and I got elected in my community. I told him sometimes people thank me and that makes it all worth it, especially when the fellow Hispanics in town thank me because I give them a voice.

He wanted to know why I was conservative and if I agreed with President Trump's decisions so far. He respected my comments and how I felt. He said, "I don't care who the president is. I just don't want our country to go to war. I just want people to be happy."

I couldn't agree more.

I told him I was getting married the next week, and he congratulated me, saying marriage is a beautiful thing. He asked, "Is he a good guy?" I said, "The best."

"How long have you been together?"

"Almost nine years."

"When it works," he said, "and you get past the good, bad, and ugly, you can achieve anything and see the stars." Then he asked, "How long have you lived in the United States?" I said, "I was little when I was adopted. About eleven months old."

Then I told him I was an aspiring writer, and he asked how far along my book was. I said several chapters. He asked about my book. I said it's going to be called something about a journey. He stopped and said, "That's great! Life is all about the journey."

When we got to my car, he said, "I'll see you on TV. God bless you. Go do big things, Amanda!"

I said goodbye, and we parted ways. I drove away and beeped as I passed him. He waved, said good luck, and gave me a thumbs up.

I was supposed to meet Lorenzo that day, and I will never forget him. I easily could have crossed to the other side of the street and avoided him.

However, I never would have learned his thoughts on marriage, politics, and life. My initial fear showed me I may have some subconscious insecurities, including a tendency to stereotype and judge a book by its cover. My challenge to you is to start a conversation with five new people each week for a month and be open to new perspectives and ideas. You never know what you will learn and whom you will cross paths with.

Exercise

1. Have you ever changed directions or avoided eye contact with someone because their appearance scared you? What might have happened if you had said hello?

_____

_____

_____

_____

2. Describe a time when you interacted with someone from a different culture or background. What did that person end up being like?

_____

_____

_____

_____

Summary

Prejudice does not happen overnight. It is learned, with each location, culture, economic division, etc. bringing its own form of ignorance and/or intolerance. It can greatly inhibit our ability to see the good in the world and in others. Every relationship and interaction happens for a reason, good or bad, either because the person will influence your future or they have a special place in your future. Remember what the Dalai Lama said, "People take different roads seeking fulfillment and happiness. Just because they're not on your road doesn't mean they've gotten lost."

If we want to improve the future, be better than those who came before us, and respect the journeys of those around us, we must look within ourselves and acknowledge the ignorance at the heart of our own biases and actions so we don't miss out on opportunities to meet new people and learn life-changing lessons.

CHAPTER 9
SETTING THE BAR HIGH

"Don't let someone else's opinion of you become your reality."

— Les Brown

In the last chapter, we talked about overcoming ignorance. Now we will talk about how to set the bar high and bring joy to your life and the lives of others. Whether it is running for office, supporting a cause, or searching for something meaningful to improve our life, we all need to find things that makes us happy. The only stipulation is we should only go after "it" if it brings us joy.

Running for Good

My stint in politics was not at all surprising. Campaigning, competing, making a difference, and being an influencer have all been in my blood since elementary school. My first campaign was in fourth grade when I ran for class president. I ended my speech with, "Vote for Amanda Doerr as your Class President. I will listen to your concerns, and I even live in a white house." Then I flashed a megawatt smile and gave a thumbs-up. I was elected as the first Orchard Hills Elementary School President by my peers. It was exciting. I would meet with my teacher Miss McAuley to help select products and run the school store.

When I was a junior in high school, I was very involved with the YMCA's Youth and Government program (YAG). This mock government club was amazing, and the students took their faux legislative responsibility seriously. Every Friday morning, we met to prepare our bills and practice debating in preparation for the annual Youth and Government Conference in Hartford, Connecticut, at the capitol building. The conference was a weekend-long event where we stayed at a hotel, took a bus to the capitol each day, and took it over as though we were the real political deal. Delegates came from all over the state, and we were very respectful of the furniture in the chambers—no food or drink other than water allowed. We were dead silent when a presiding officer or anyone was speaking, and we were respectful of each other's feelings and viewpoints even on the most contentious bills presented and debated on the floor.

During this YAG weekend, a friend of mine convinced me to run for the lieutenant governor position. Normally, people came to the conference prepared and knowing they would be running for an office. However, I like to walk on the wild side and go with my gut even if it might seem crazy and overly optimistic. I decided to run, jotting my speech down on a napkin during lunch because speeches and voting were in the afternoon. I walked around the cafeteria campaigning and introducing myself to anyone who looked at me.

Later that day, I was ready to give my speech to 300 students and, hopefully, get elected. About twenty minutes before giving my speech, I realized I couldn't find it. I took a deep breath and quickly wrote some bullet points from what I had written. I was confident and told myself if I didn't win, it wasn't the end of the world. But if I did win, it would look amazing on my resume.

When it was my turn to speak, I crushed it. I hit all my major talking points, spoke about my experience in YAG, and expressed my desire to improve the following year's conference and ensure the program would be as successful as it could be.

I am pleased to say I was elected, and it was a great experience that took me to Asheville, North Carolina, to attend the YMCA Conference On National Affairs (CONA). The following January, I presided over a YAG session in the real Connecticut Senate Chambers, maintaining order and using Robert's Rules of Order, and I loved every minute of it. These experiences would later set the stage for my real political run.

Exercise

1. If you ventured into politics, what position would you run for?

_____

_____

_____

_____

_____

_____

2. What extracurricular activity or class in high school made the biggest difference in your life?

_____

_____

_____

_____

Supporting Freedom

I find it fitting that we have several holidays throughout the year that recognize those who fight to protect our freedom internationally and domestically. Memorial Day, Veteran's Day, and First Responders Day are just a few. First responders and military personnel truly are heroes and deserve the utmost respect.

My grandfather, Elmer Doerr, was an exceptionally resilient and determined person. He was the quiet type, so when he did talk, it was worth listening to. He joined the army during World War II, causing him to be away from my grandmother for three years. He was stationed in England and served in France, Germany, and Holland. His job was driving the trucks that carried the pontoon boats. When my grandfather came back from World War II, his love for the red, white, and blue never faltered. Serving the country and being American made him extremely proud. Not a day went by that the American flag wasn't waving on the pole in his yard.

As he got older, my grandfather's mind remained sharp. At ninety-two, he still drove and did his best to maintain his hobbies. At ninety-six, he didn't let health issues hold him back; he always bounced back from any malady like a champ. At the end of his life, his patriotism was still apparent. He was given an American Flag pin and wore it every day until the day he passed on at age ninety-eight on December 26, 2015.

My brother Nate is a Marine and police officer. He has dedicated his life to protecting and serving others. When we were kids, we used to play cops and robbers all the time. Guess who was the robber? I would steal my own Pretty Pretty Princess jewelry. Nate would always catch me and make me put it back. I would then go to jail or the box, which was the hall coat closet. This was the worst part about playing with my brother because I hated dark and confined spaces. I vowed never to get in trouble and go to jail. Nate taught me I always want to be on the right side of the law.

It was evident from a young age

that Nate would go into the military. More often than not, he was rockin' camo, crawling on the ground, doing spin moves, and playing with toy guns and GI Joe. It was as if God had handpicked him to protect and serve.

Nate joined the United States Marine Corp reserves in his early twenties. A year later, he was deployed. Prior to being deployed, he was one step away from getting his dream job as a law enforcement patrol officer. Fortunately, the Milford Police Department put his position on hold until he returned.

Nate served in Bahrain, United Arab Emirates, and Okinawa in Japan. While at the police academy, he received the prestigious Allen J. Tuskowski Award given to the person at the top of the class for excellence in all areas of police training. His desire to pursue a career in law enforcement stemmed from the same patriotism and respect for the United States that had inspired him to enlist in the Marine Corp.

I have always admired Gramps and Nate's strength and discipline. I will never forget their quirky goofy sides. The coolest thing of all is that they both dedicated time to serving our country, something not everyone has the strength to do. Without individuals like these two, and the many other brave men and women all over the United States, we would not have the luxuries and freedoms we have today. Appreciate and salute the heroes keeping us safe. Next time you see a police officer, or an active duty or retired veteran, thank them for their service. A thank you for a hard job goes a long way!

Exercise

1. If you had to join a branch of the military, which would you choose and why?

   _____

   _____

   _____

   _____

2. What do you want your life to look like when you are in your nineties?

   _____

   _____

   _____

   _____

Practicing Mind Over Body

Have you ever been insecure about your appearance? I am not talking about a blemish on your nose but insecurity about a physical attribute like a skin disorder or something that visibly sets you apart and makes you uncomfortable?

Nick Santonastasso is an amazing young man who hasn't let his rare condition affect his morale or ambition. Nick was born with Hanhart syndrome, which is very rare. The few people who have this condition have limbs that do not fully develop.

In a podcast interview, Santonastasso discussed body image insecurity. He explained that food and fitness are fuel, and thinking positively can help us be better, more successful people. He said if someone doesn't want to connect on an intimate level because of the other person's body, the body acts as an organic filter, weeding out those who are not worth our time and energy. This is a positive way of looking at life, relationships, and our bodies.

Santonastasso has helped millions, and he has done so because of the encouragement and independence his parents gave him. When he was young, his parents knew his life would not be easy, but like any good parent would, they wanted him to be able to fend for himself. We all need to teach our children to be independent when they are young so they can be successful adults.

Pushing kids to be independent and then essentially pushing them out of the nest may seem harsh, but it is a big reason Santonastasso is so resilient and seeks adventure. Despite his disability, he doesn't make excuses. He explores and tries new things like wrestling, skateboarding, modeling, bodybuilding, and public speaking. This man does not accept limits and has developed a confidence of steel. He has truly found his calling, and he successfully inspires people to look at the world differently.

Exercise

1. What do you love about your appearance?

_____

_____

_____

_____

2. What physical activity do you want to try but have made excuses to avoid?

_____

_____

_____

_____

Summary

Setting the bar high doesn't happen overnight. Follow someone who inspires you so you can learn new things, pursue new opportunities, and assume a new role. Be unstoppable and always remember to send the elevator down by mentoring, inspiring, and being at the service of others. Go on—make a difference in others' lives by doing what you are meant to do: set the bar high, exceed your dreams, and take control of your destiny.

CHAPTER 10
OWNING YOUR MISTAKES

"Mistakes are always forgivable if one has the courage to admit them."

— Bruce Lee

In the last chapter, we talked about setting the bar high. This chapter is all about embracing your mistakes. Not only the big mistakes, but the small mistakes that can end up being an important milestone on the way to an important next step. Most of the time, a mistake teaches us something great, and if we learn from it, we won't make the same mistake twice.

Forgiving Debt

Have you ever struggled financially or made a big purchase like a car or house, then felt the heat of the suffocating debt? Debt, bills, and taxes suck.... I think I covered it all, right? These three financial burdens are part of everyday life, but only one is avoidable. If you play your cards right and make smart money choices, you guessed it, you can avoid debt!

Turning eighteen comes with many responsibilities: voting rights, ability to get a credit card (or four if you are like me), a tattoo or piercing without your parents' consent, being able to play the lottery, and some other things depending on the state. I made the mistake of getting my belly button pierced at a place that totally botched it and left a nasty scar.

However, the biggest mistake for a shopaholic like me was getting jobs and credit cards at retail stores, especially stores I shopped at regularly. Of course, I set the goal of only buying a few things and paying off the card with my paycheck. However, most of the retail stores I worked at encouraged employees not only to wear the clothes the store sold because it made it easier to sell, but they also encouraged us to take advantage of the credit card savings. They gave us 50 percent off our first purchase as employees if we opened a charge account and used the card. So, if you bought $1,000 worth of clothes, you would pay $500, which was a great deal, but who needs that many clothes? A young shopaholic who doesn't know better and thinks she needs that many clothes, that's who.

Have you ever pondered the difference between a want and a need?

In any case, if you want or need something, pay in cash.

It doesn't matter how much money you make—what matters is how much you keep.

Credit cards can be an important step in building credit and learning responsibility. However, a retail credit card typically has a super-high interest rate. For certain people, like me, the world of instantaneous purchases can become addicting, and if you don't have the cash available, it can be disastrous to your psyche and future. I should know. I broke many of the cardinal rules of responsible credit card use. I selected high-interest retail cards, bought things knowing I couldn't pay for them in that moment, and paid $5,000 plus in college tuition and books with a card. To make matters worse, I carried a balance.

I was able to recover and pay off my debt in my twenties, but it came at a price and cost me valuable time and considerable mental anguish. I now have a credit score above 800, so it is possible to get your financial stats back in order with a game plan and dedication.

If you set a financial goal and use the financial tools and resources at your fingertips, you can succeed. For example, once you pay off credit card debt, you can invest that money. If you start investing small sums while simultaneously educating yourself on stocks, you can invest in a calculated way. If you create a budget and purchase products and services in a calculated way, you will not blow through your money. The goal is to have a plan, mitigate risk by diversifying your investments and limiting credit card use.

Even though debt, bills, taxes, and other financial issues still cause stress from time to time, I have learned the importance of budgeting, limiting certain purchases to certain cards so it is easier to track, not carrying a balance, and really being intentional about purchasing items that bring me joy and add value to my life.

Regardless of your financial situation, I want you to smile, take a deep breath, and repeat after me. "Behind every financial burden or poor decision lies an opportunity to learn and do better." So be positive, make a financial plan, and try your best to stick to it. Your wallet and future will thank you later.

Exercise

1. List five ways you can cut back on spending.

    _____

    _____

    _____

    _____

    _____

2. Have you ever made a purchase you regretted or didn't end up using? Why did you originally buy the item?

    _____

    _____

    _____

    _____

    _____

Overcoming Bad Habits and Growing an Empire

Have you ever fallen into a rut where it felt like your world was going to crash and burn? It can happen to anyone, and most people have dark periods, but the light after the darkness can be just around the corner with a little bit of hope, faith, and the right support.

My friend and fellow University of New Haven alum, Don Fertman, is most recently known for being the chief development officer of Subway and John Wilson on *Undercover Boss*. First, he was actively involved in the music scene on campus at the University of New Haven. He was a WNHU disc jockey and formed a band called the Crayons. He was known as the orange crayon. He became connected with Subway when asked to create a jingle for the brand. Fertman went on to become friends with Fred DeLuca, the founder of Subway, and worked for Subway for thirty-nine years.

Fertman is a great and very successful man, but like most of us, his journey didn't come without challenges. He overcame alcohol and cocaine habits to help grow Subway to what it is today. He attributes much of his success to his mentor, the late Fred DeLuca, who saw something great in Fertman and was willing to support him throughout his recovery. This support was tremendously important to his road to recovery.

Now retired, Fertman gives back to causes dear to his heart—Brave Enough to Fail, a Connecticut-based educational nonprofit that provides free motivational programs, resources, and scholarships to middle and high schools, and The Phoenix, an organization working to build a sober, active community that fuels resilience and harnesses the transformational power of connection so together we rise, recover, and live. Like a phoenix rising from the ashes, this organization gives people a second shot at life after recovery.

It is quite amazing when people take their hardships and low points and use them to help make others' lives better. Fertman's story is inspiring, and he is a beacon of hope for those who are struggling.

Exercise

1. Which bad habit could you eliminate to improve your health and financial situation?

    _____

    _____

    _____

    _____

2. If you could be on the executive team or board of any company in the world, which would it be?

    _____

    _____

    _____

    _____

3. If you could do anything in retirement, what would you do?

    _____

    _____

    _____

    _____

Vacuuming Failure

Are you familiar with the top vacuum brands on the market today? I have personally felt the power and cleaning ability of the Dyson, and although it is pricey, it does not disappoint if you have pets, messy children, or just like your home to be extremely clean.

James Dyson is a British inventor who created the Dyson vacuum. He first thought of it back in 1978 when he became frustrated with the performance of his vacuum cleaner. He took it apart and realized the bag kept clogging with dust. This bottleneck caused suction to drop, which ruined the vacuum's performance. It took Dyson fifteen years and 5,127 prototypes to create what we now know as the Dual Cyclone vacuum, the world's first bagless vacuum cleaner.

Dyson believes that creativity comes from failure. His failure resulted in a multi-billion-dollar company.

Are you willing to stare failure in the face, smile, and say "Thanks for letting me know there is a better way"? Would you then keep trying, or give up, not knowing you were on the precipice of success?

Exercise

1. Describe a situation when a failure turned into a success.

    _____

    _____

    _____

2. What innovation would make your daily routine easier?

_____

_____

_____

_____

Learning from Mistakes

No matter how old you are, you most likely have heard of, if not used Netflix. Netflix has been around for twenty-four years, and despite some uncertainty caused by poor decisions early on, it doesn't appear to be going anywhere. Other entertainment brands, however, have had some success and then tapped out over the years.

Blockbuster opened in 1985, and within three years, it dominated the video chain industry; at one point, it even expanded into the global market. Unfortunately, a few missteps and an inability to bend with the times led to its bankruptcy in 2010; eventually, all its corporate run stores closed by 2014 after a failed attempt to launch an online DVD rental service.

In 1998, Netflix started out with a DVD-by-mail subscription service. Although it was a simple idea, it continued to adapt and grow, and today, it offers options that entertain 207 million subscribers. Back in 2000, Netflix owner Reed Hastings offered to sell Netflix to Blockbuster CEO John Antioco for $50 million. Antioco declined. One decision can make or break a company.

Exercise

1. What major failed company sticks out most in your mind?

    _____

    _____

    _____

    _____

2. How can you learn from your mistakes to be more successful in the future?

    _____

    _____

    _____

    _____

Summary

Mistakes are only negative if you continue to make the same ones. Failure and mistakes can lead to innovation, solutions, and progress. The greatest lessons often come from failure because we learn more from our mistakes. Don't beat yourself up when you fall short because it may open the door to the next big thing for you.

CHAPTER 11
EMBRACING FAMILY CHANGES

"A hundred years from now it will not matter what my bank account
was, the sort of house I lived in, or the kind of car I drove...but the
world may be different because I was important in the life of a child."

— Forest E. Witcraft

In the last chapter, we talked about owning our mistakes whether they
lead to good or bad outcomes. Now let's talk about something most people really have a hard time with—how the world changes when you decide to create your own family. Whether it is a family of two, three, four, or more, change is guaranteed, so never stop moving forward and evolving and do so while giving yourself some very important grace and patience.

Giving Grace to Motherhood

Motherhood has and will continue to consume me and be the biggest, hardest, and best change of my life. From pregnancy and miscarriage to pregnancy again, labor, and postpartum healing, the pain, emotions, and hormones can be overwhelming. Before I got pregnant with Luca, I miscarried. It was difficult for Pete and me and put a strain on our marriage. He didn't understand the loss and pain I felt, and I didn't know how to explain it to him. I still feel sadness every October when he or she was lost and every June when he or she would have been born, but I maintained hope that things happen for a reason.

Then we had my rainbow baby, Luca. For the first two-and-a-half years of his life, I had the privilege to spend a lot of time with him. We were together nearly all day every day while Pete worked in Rhode Island and came home on the weekends. However, the same challenging year Luca was born, I also had several major things happen:

- I took a new job at Edible Arrangements while pregnant.
- Peter took a new job out of state.
- I experienced a mass layoff.
- We had marital struggles.
- I spent time recovering from major surgery (a C-section).
- We had our first child.
- We prepared to move to a new state.
- I developed an autoimmune disease called Hashimoto's disease.
- I started consulting and taking on clients two months postpartum.

This was a depressing time, and sometimes I truly thought I wouldn't survive. However, the move to Rhode Island was a fresh start and changed my attitude about the future. That is when magic began to happen: I started a gratitude journal; we got a new bank; we bought some stuff for the new house; and we began focusing on this new chapter together under one roof. This was our second chance at marriage, our second chance to create a positive and better family. The family our son and future children deserved. I took back my health and began investing in me and my family. More importantly, I forgave and let go of the resentment that had become a squatter in my heart.

One day, I was getting dressed to take Luca to the Impossible Dream playground in Warwick, Rhode Island. It is one of the top-rated playgrounds in the country. It is ADA compliant and an amazing spot for kids. We had lunch and a playdate scheduled with Luca's little girlfriend Ellie and her mom Kristen, who became a dear friend. As a working mom and business owner, sometimes making friends is hard. I am often very busy and sometimes can't fully relate to stay-at-home moms since I am a hybrid between a CEO and a mama. On the days I had Luca at home, I tried to work half the day and play the rest, so we got some time in, and I took this time very seriously. Spending time with my family is non-negotiable for me.

Anyway, as I was getting ready, all of a sudden, I heard Luca's little voice calling for help. He walked into the room with his face covered in brown smears. I flinched and immediately thought he had wiped poop, finger-paint-style, all over his little cherub face. "Ah! bub, what did you do?" I half-scolded. "Is it poopy?"

"No, Mommy, not poopy…chocolate, and it was delicious!" Luca beckoned me to follow him, but I already knew he had gotten into the box of chocolates I had prepared as a client thank you gift.

We walked downstairs where Luca pointed to chocolate gold coin wrappers strewn everywhere and the melted chocolate all over the tan leather couch. I took him to the sink and angrily cleaned off his face, telling him never to touch Mommy's work things, and if he were hungry, he needed to ask first.

I said we were supposed to be at the playdate but would now be late because I had to clean up the mess. I was not calm, and I am embarrassed that I was so mean in the moment. I was angry about having the nice afternoon I had planned for him ruined by having to clean up his mess.

Today, this story makes me both happy and sad as I picture Luca's smiling and guilty chocolate-smeared face. Remembering the mess on the couch and the gold foil wrappers everywhere makes me chuckle now. However, I feel a pang of guilt because I can still hear my son sobbing as I grabbed him and yelled about the mess and mistake he had made. He kept saying, "Sorry I messed up, Mommy."

The mom-guilt from when I lost my temper or had to juggle work and mother-son time really weighed on me, so I started spending purposeful time with Luca and not sweating the small stuff or messes because things happen and I knew my time with him while he was young was fleeting. Since his little brother was born and Luca turned three, he has become less and less dependent on me, which makes me happy and sad.

In case you were wondering, the couch turned out fine, there was enough chocolate to go around, and we went to all our planned activities and had fun. The moral of this story is: Be kind to the little growing humans you love—no material thing or appointment on your calendar is worth hurting their feelings over, and no event is more important than your little loves.

Exercise

1. What qualities make a great mother? What qualities make a great father? How many of these qualities do you possess?

   _____

   _____

   _____

   _____

2. What anger or resentment are you holding in your heart? Write it down and rip it up, burn it, etc. Whatever you need to do to physically discard it will serve you well.

   _____

   _____

   _____

   _____

Raising the Future

Growing a family is one of the biggest changes people ever experience. Whether it is through birth, adoption, or being a rockstar auntie or uncle, it is the hardest job and can be the biggest and most wonderful disruption to your life. It can also be filled with joy, heartbreak, exhaustion, and grief for those of you who, like me, have lost a baby.

To believe in someone else, you must first believe in yourself, which makes me believe my adoptive mom really must have had a lot of confidence to take the journey she did. We are not all nature. Nurture plays a huge role in who we become and how we get there. When I was little, I spent a lot of time with my mom, and I am blessed for it. The older I get, the more I realize I have learned so much from my mom that has helped me in life. Here is a list of some of those things:

1. **Bribery**, or incentive as I like to refer to it, helps to reinforce lessons and make them stick better in a little person's mind. I used to judge parents who used this tactic; however, now I use this parenting technique when it's called for. I now know firsthand how difficult being a parent is. So, I now know an M&M incentive here and there isn't detrimental to children's development.

2. **Candor**, or as I call it, tell it like it is. My mom wears her heart on her sleeve. If something is wrong, you know. If something is good, you know. Like my mom, I am honest and have no filter. I tell it like it is and believe transparency and honesty are of the utmost importance—this has served me well.

3. **Philanthropy** and giving back to better the world. My mom is a chronic do-gooder, and I love her for it. She taught me the importance of giving, donating time, and being aware of others. Through her experiences combined with my own experiences, I learned to think outside of my four walls and appreciate being an American in the United States. She has experienced some very poor countries and knows that no matter what you are going through, life is always harder for someone else

and that we always have things to be grateful for.

4. **Priorities** should be adhered to. My mom has always put family first, an important lesson I didn't always get when I was younger, especially in high school. However, the older I get, the more reverent and clear this lesson has become because family really is the driving force for everything for me—more specifically, my children and my niece Aubrey and nephews Bryce, Sammy and Cooper. The children are the future, and everything I do is for them.

5. **Education** is very important. My mom is an educator, and although she is retired, she is still willing and ready to teach others, especially if they want to learn Spanish. She taught me the importance of being educated, continuing to learn, and being willing to teach others. She always taught in a fun way that inspires me to teach others in the same manner to honor her.

I visualized who I would become, and I know there is still more work to do to get there, but I have faith that what I've been through will help me along my journey and may inspire and help others going through similar scenarios. I do not know exactly how my life will play out, but I know I have a purpose.

I also know you have your own special, natural gifts to share, so don't let society, media, or people with no vision take away those dreams. I had a mother who told me throughout my childhood to *dream bigger* and that I could do anything I want, so I am! I want you not only to dream bigger, but to get out and share all that nurture and nature has given you. And if you haven't been blessed with the lessons I have learned or the nurturing I was blessed with, you can still consciously and proactively give what you haven't received as a gift to enrich others' lives.

Exercise

1. What is your earliest memory of someone or yourself believing you could do something?

   _____

   _____

   _____

   _____

2. What was the biggest change you went through?

   _____

   _____

   _____

   _____

Getting Hitched

Marriage is a special vow, but it is also one of the hardest relationships you will have. Anyone who says marriage is easy is full of it because it is the merger of two different minds, two different upbringings, and two separate journeys coming together to live as one. That is why doing your best to select the right partner, whether for a business venture or a marriage, is an important decision not to be taken lightly.

It was an ordinary college day; I was getting ready for Mr. Marciano's English lit class, and I was with a friend from class killing some time. On a whim, we decided to go to a local tattoo shop. I got my belly button repierced—which was yet again a terrible idea—and she got her nose pierced. We then bumped into her dormmate. He was kind of cute. She told him we had just gotten piercings and showed off her nose ring. I lifted my shirt to show my belly button. In hindsight, this was a terrible idea because this guy was a stranger to me—and it turned out he hated belly buttons.

He asked if he could bum a ride to Harugari Hall, one of the buildings with classrooms, and it just so happened we all had the same class. My friend, of course, said yes, if he didn't mind a pit stop at McDonald's.

After a few days of class, I decided I wanted this cute, older guy to myself. I passed him a note asking him on a date. I asked him if he wanted to go out that night and left empty check boxes below—one for yes and one for no. He checked yes, and the rest is history.

Nine years later, the day of our wedding started off sunny. Per usual, the women were up at the crack of dawn primping and getting dressed. The men rolled out of bed, relaxed, and took their sweet time grabbing beverages and throwing on their suits. June 30, 2017, was the day I would marry my college sweetheart Peter. Yes, he was the one who hates belly buttons, but

apparently mine didn't deter him from dating me for nine years. We selected the most perfect and beautiful venue, Wood Acres—a Clydesdale horse
farm in northwestern Connecticut. The venue is stunning and rustic, perfectly suited for our Southern BBQ-style menu and watermelon margaritas.

Although the morning was sunny, the weather report called for torrential
downpours. Go figure. Of course, it was one of the biggest days of my life.
Well, my glass half full side said at least I was not stuck on a mountain.
(Note, this reference has to do with the upcoming Chapter 17: Climbing
Your Mountains.) Some things money can't buy, and good weather for an
event is one of them. Trust me, I asked when we booked the venue. We
were fortunate to get some stunning photos and have an outdoor ceremony
with no rain but enough thunder to scare Poseidon.

Unlike with my Youth and Government election speech, I did not lose my
vows, but I did wait until the last minute to write them. I snuck away for
a few minutes during the rehearsal and jotted them down in a bathroom
stall. I work well under pressure. I strategically stored them in my bra so I
wouldn't have to wing it.

As a big sports fan and a fan of analogies and puns, can you guess what my
vows were about? Yes, football, of course! Check them out:

> Peter, you are my best friend and my wingman; you are my rock when
> there's a tough play and my protector when there's a blitz. On offense,
> you are the equivalent to my Antonio Brown, and I vow to be your Big
> Ben. I will cheer you on, throw you solid passes, respect your routes,
> and cherish your catches. I will be there not only to help you celebrate

the wins but to recover from the losses, and most of all, I vow to love you for all the days of my life.

Our wedding day was quite special, and we had a blast despite the torrential downpour and miscellaneous things that didn't go according to plan. It was a lot like marriage. We all have ups and downs and in betweens, but that is what makes the marital relationship so special. We are still getting to know each other, learning from each other, and trying to get into a flow, especially with the addition of two kiddos. We will always have our differences, our lovers' spats, and times we want to strangle each other, but that is what makes things interesting.

Like entrepreneurship, the lows are low, and the highs are high; the wins and the happy moments make up for the not-so-great moments. Sometimes, the greatest things in life don't come easy, and I am okay with that. I don't know what the future holds, but we will take it day by day and always have a place for each other in our hearts.

Exercise

1. How did you react the last time things didn't go to plan?

    _____

    _____

    _____

    _____

2. What can you actively do to make your personal and professional relationships more successful?

    _____

    _____

    _____

    _____

Summary

Whatever family change is thrown your way, you will eventually adjust and evolve, whether the change is for the best or not. In the moment, rest assured it will allow for future reflection and personal growth, which is always a good thing. My advice is to always take the time to learn, love, and laugh with the ones you love because no matter what, life is fragile, and we only get so much time together. If you aren't seeing positive results, get your mind right and roll with the change—continue writing your journey and fostering your legacy. Keep evolving, my friend, and make sure you focus on what matters most!

CHAPTER 12
EMPOWERING YOUR SOUL

"Surround yourself with people who make you stronger and better."

— Julia Hartz

In the last chapter, we talked about how change can affect your life. Now we will discuss how to empower your soul. This chapter will give you all the good feelings, so cozy up with a warm beverage, a soft blanket, and reflect on your hopes and dreams. Just do me a favor and throw your fear and doubt into the fire.

Celebrating the "Gotcha Day"

Have you ever heard of a "Gotcha Day"? This is a special holiday celebrated by many furry and human adoptees all over the world to celebrate the day they were "got." Adoption is something so special, but it can also be very stressful and cause stress and anxiety throughout the adoptee's life.

On December 17, 2014, I was getting ready for work and the day ahead. Trying to decide quickly on my work outfit, I settled for some skinny jeans, even though I was feeling a bit bloated, and a loose-fitting white blouse with a leather fur vest. I put on my comfy flats and grabbed a pair of high-heeled boots to change into. I left a little bit later than I wanted, but I was still the first person at work and got a few things done before my boss came in. I was trying to get everything I possibly could done before 4 p.m. when I was supposed to leave. I banged out a couple of presentations and followed up on my orders without a hitch.

Around 3 p.m., my mom called. She sounded kind of funny. I instantly thought someone had died and she was about to tell me. When I asked if everything was okay, she said, "Yes, but did you forget what today is?" I had absolutely no idea where she was going with this and said, "Nope." She then told me it was my Gotcha Day and she had a present for me. I slapped my forehead because I had completely forgotten my parents "got" me twenty-three years earlier on that day. The whole premise of celebrating my Gotcha Day is that it signifies my rebirth as a Doerr. Since my mother didn't give birth to me, this was her way of telling the world and me that this baby, young girl, and now grown woman is hers and will always be hers.

When I was younger, she used to come to my elementary school and bring donuts or cupcakes to celebrate. This was wonderful for me because my birthday typically fell on Martin Luther King, Jr. Day or on a snow day, so I couldn't celebrate with my class. December 17 was a second chance for me to have a special day and celebrate with some sweet treats and my classmates. Mom always took the opportunity to explain adoption, my Hispanic heritage, and how I was part of our family, even though I wasn't born in the United States. This explanation became more and more important each year because my peers had questions like "Why don't you look like your parents?" or "Why were you adopted?"

This celebration was so much more than dessert—it was an opportunity for me to feel normal and for my classmates to understand me better. It creates beautiful memories that touch my soul and remind me of how much my parents love me and how much I appreciate my unique story.

Later that day, my mom popped into my office, gave me a little gift certificate, and hugged me. The gift card to ULTA was the perfect thing to get my cosmetic fix, so I headed there after work. I maneuvered through the displays to the register in the front of the store. I was next in line, so the cashier motioned for me to come forward, and I placed my pretty pink lipsticks and sparkly eyeshadows on the counter. I told her the gift card was from my mom for my Gotcha Day. She asked what a Gotcha Day was, and I said I was adopted from South America and every year my parents celebrate the day they officially got me. Her eyes teared up, and she said, "I appreciate you sharing your story and your positive outlook."

Then she told me, "I was adopted, and I hate my life." I felt the pain of her words in my heart because I knew that not everyone's situation is as happy as mine. I purchased my new makeup goodies, thanked her for helping me, and told her I hoped the rest of her day would be wonderful. Although I couldn't take away her pain or erase her bad life experiences, sometimes smiling and being kind can make a positive difference in someone else's day, even if it is just temporary. I hope she found happiness.

This and several other interactions with various people have caused me to want to adopt a child and give them the love they deserve—and to prevent someone else from being hurt like this woman had been.

Sometimes life is so busy that we lose sight of the moments and the people who bring us joy. As the years pass, those people may leave our lives, so it is vital to cherish them while they are with us. Remember, not everyone has as many special moments as you, so reflect upon and cherish the events and people who make your life special. And don't be afraid to show compassion for others—strangers need love too.

Exercise

1. Describe a special moment in your life that made you feel accepted and loved.

    _____

    _____

    _____

    _____

    _____

2. I always keep extra water bottles and snacks in my car to give to the homeless. Is there something you can do today to be a good neighbor?

    _____

    _____

    _____

    _____

    _____

Seeking Answers

Have you ever received an Amber Alert on your phone? As a parent, when I get one, it sends chills down my spine and scary thoughts through my head as I pray for the missing child's safe return.

Children, especially those who can't recall their last name, let alone where they live, may never find their way home if they get lost or abducted. The movie *The Lion* shines a light on this scenario; a five-year-old boy in India gets lost on a train and ends up awakening alone in a major city. Not knowing his full name, where he lives, or his mother's name, he is immediately lost in the abyss of Kolkata. He roams around trying to get help, but he is ignored because people think he is a homeless beggar and beneath their attention. He eventually ends up in an orphanage and is adopted by an Australian couple.

The movie really touched my soul. Not only because I am now a mother and can't imagine losing a child, but I also know what it feels like to think you are unwanted and forgotten and to grow up far from your birth country within a family that isn't your nationality. The themes expressed in the movie reflect common situations with foreign adoption. Much of what the boy felt about being adopted is very relatable, and similar sentiments are regularly expressed in adoption groups.

With the invention of Google Earth, the boy is able to go in search of his family and return to his first home. This story makes the world feel a bit more cozy and less vast. The internet has allowed connections and family histories to be discovered through the click of a button. Facebook is how I ended up finding some of my biological family members and how I currently keep in contact with them. The internet is a powerful and robust tool so use it wisely.

Exercise

1. Have you explored your family history or learned anything new about family members by searching online? Google yourself. What did you find?

    _____

    _____

    _____

    _____

2. Where is your family from? If you have never been there, I challenge you to use Google Earth to visit virtually.

    _____

    _____

    _____

    _____

Believing in Above

The end of high school is often stress-ridden. Graduation is a major milestone, a time when we decide what to do with our lives—or at least which college we will attend. We are faced with one of life's biggest decisions since we spend most of our lives working. What do you do with your life? What college or career path is best? And will you be able to provide for your future?

One summer day a few weeks before I started my senior year, I was attending an ACT study course. I wasn't really excelling at it, so I was concerned not only about how I would do on my SAT/ACT but also how my music school auditions would go. It was a stunningly beautiful summer day, with not one cloud in the crystal-blue sky. The class couldn't end quickly enough for me. When we were released, I hopped in my mom's Volvo station wagon, which she had let me borrow, and decided to take a detour and go to the tanning salon.

I had some sessions left, and I figured my mom wouldn't miss her Volvo for another thirty minutes. I couldn't help but feel a pang of guilt, though, because my mom had skin cancer on her face, and she did not condone tanning. However, I was a selfish and invincible teenager, so I thought, *C'est la vie.* Fortunately, tracking your kid's movement through Find My Phone wasn't a thing yet. I got my dose of UV rays and headed home.

It was about 11 a.m., and I was sitting at a light when my phone started buzzing. I glance down and saw the caller ID—Mom. Ugh. I groaned and almost didn't answer as the guilt overcame me. I thought maybe she had been with my dad at the IGA next door to the tanning place and had caught me.

Mom sounded strange, and my fight-or-flight reaction immediately kicked in. I pulled into the Robert Treat Park parking lot. What followed was one of the worst moments of my life. She calmly explained that my dad was in the ICU. The bruise we had found on his neck the day before had created a large hematoma under his tongue, which closed his throat. Later, we learned the hematoma had been caused by an allergic reaction triggered by the combination of his Coumadin blood thinner medication and an antibiotic.

I thought it was a joke at first…all right Ashton Kutcher, cue the *Punked* cameras. I mean it couldn't be real, right? My heart was pounding, and I could feel the tears welling up behind my eyes. Mom said not to come to the hospital, so I hesitantly went home.

Mom called around four to tell me Dad was in surgery. I lost it again. I don't know which was worse—the waiting or thinking about maybe having to say goodbye to my dad. Up until July 29, 2006, life was going as planned, and then in the blink of an eye, my world came tumbling down.

I arrived at Yale New Haven Hospital to find my dad hooked up to all kinds of machines. I lost it yet again because I hardly recognized him. All I could think was it couldn't be him. Seeing a loved one suffer in such a sterile and scary environment is torture, especially when all you can do is wait, pray, and watch. The ICU was not like it is on *Grey's Anatomy*—it was too real, and I had no idea what the script said next. I was at a loss for words, so I kind of wished I had a script to read from.

My dad is a good man. Sometimes we don't always see eye to eye or bond on a purely emotional level because I am so sensitive, but he's a big part of my life. Why was he lying in the ICU? It didn't seem fair; he went to church, volunteered, worked hard, and loved his family. All I could do for him was hold his hand, and that didn't feel like nearly enough. He was barely moving and couldn't speak because of the tube down his throat. We wrote to each other on a notepad to communicate. He said we should fix my brother up with the cute nurse. I laughed and couldn't have agreed more. Even in pain and not knowing if he would live, my dad was still joking. He got that from my Gramps.

I couldn't shake the guilty feeling about going to the tanning salon. Was I being punished by the universe for being a bratty, selfish teen? I would gladly give up tanning or work hard at being a better, more honest, and respectful daughter if that would allow God to help heal my dad. In that moment, I needed to be alone and cry, and I needed to cry hard, so I excused myself from the room to spare my mom from feeling like she needed to console me. She had enough to worry about. I couldn't imagine being in her shoes, not knowing if you are about to lose your husband. Thinking about all the memories and love, I felt tears streaming down my face.

While sitting in the lobby by the fountain, I felt bad for not being by my dad's side, but I needed a little space to think, appreciate life, and pray for him. As I listened and sobbed to "Butterfly Kisses" by Bob Carlisle, the song I selected for our father-daughter dance at my future wedding, I wondered if my dad would overcome this illness and be with me on my wedding day.

I headed back to the room. As I did, I saw a placard on a door to my left labelled Priest. I knew exactly what I had to do next. I needed to pray harder than I ever had before, so I knocked on the door and asked the priest if he would say a prayer for my dad even though we were Lutheran. He said,

"Of course," and sat me down, held my hand, and prayed with me. I prayed with all my heart that my dad would be okay. Looking back, this was one of my biggest prayers ever—and it was answered!

My dad recovered fully from his scary allergic reaction. One of the first things I bought him after was a mocha shake—he had scribbled a request on the notepad while he was in the hospital. Now, whenever I order a mocha anything, I think about those scary few days and how different my life could have been if we had lost him then.

The feelings I had at the hospital will be forever ingrained in my brain. Life is so precious, and we never know when someone we love will fall ill or pass away. Be present, love unconditionally, and don't take life too seriously even when times get tough.

Exercise

1. I challenge you to reach out to your parents, brothers, sisters, and other family members today to tell them you are thinking of them. It doesn't have to be a long-winded call, text, or email—if you are an old soul like me, snail mail works too—just a simple check in to connect.

2. Describe a time you or a loved one went to the hospital for an emergency.

_____

_____

_____

_____

Listening to Your Soul

One way to listen to your soul is to stop talking and listen. Whether the advice you get from your inner voice pertains to business or your personal life, make sure you listen because your inner voice is vital to being successful. Quieting your thoughts and words and embracing quiet meditation can work wonders for your happiness, productivity, and wellbeing.

The year 2020 was a tumultuous one to say the least, but sometimes from a disorderly and confusing time comes a beautiful silver lining. Stressful, uncertain times also bring forth the true colors of a leader for the better or sometimes the worst. If the leader or organization is willing to put others' needs at the forefront of decisions even during uncertain times, then breakthroughs and productivity can soar.

Randomly one evening, my husband Peter approached me about participating in a program his company, Jensen Hughes, was offering their employees. It was an optional and complimentary *Positive Intelligence* (PQ) course by the *New York Times* best-selling author Shazard Charmine.

Charmine is well-qualified to teach about intelligence. He has a PhD in neuroscience, a BA in psychology, an MS in electrical engineering, and an MBA from Stanford. He lectures at Stanford and guides graduates through his popular six-week PQ course. He also provides this PQ training to hundreds of executive teams all over. Charmine believes, "Your mind is your best friend. But it can also be your worst enemy."

Charmine's program dives into some breakthrough research and the various saboteurs that plague our minds. Saboteurs include the:

- Avoider
- Controller
- Hyper-Achiever
- Hyper-Rational
- Hyper-Vigilant
- Pleaser
- Restless
- Stickler
- Victim

The PQ training was very beneficial during a time when many people were feeling scared, isolated, confused, and overwhelmed. It is very admirable that Jensen Hughes took the steps to proactively extend this opportunity to their employees and their family members to help curb the angst and negative mental health effects of a pandemic. Personally, Peter and I used the six-week program to reflect on our own personal saboteurs and how best to be patient with each other.

Everyone is fighting their own saboteurs, so be kind and patient, especially during times of uncertainty and stress.

Exercise

1. Actively spend ten minutes each day this week being silent and listening to your breath and the sounds around you. Cherish this time alone with yourself and clear your mind. How did it feel to take a pause?

_____

_____

_____

_____

2. Reflecting on your day, who and what are you grateful for?

_____

_____

_____

_____

3. Which saboteurs are you fighting?

_____

_____

_____

_____

Living Like a Stoic

I have developed an appreciation for stoicism and a keen liking for the historical philosophers who lived it. Life is hard, and I see nothing wrong with providing ourselves with an arsenal of mental weapons to combat the challenges afflicting our bodies, minds, and souls.

Stoicism is a meditative way of thinking that suppresses negative thoughts and emotions. As emotional beings, stoicism is best for decision making, living in a good mental state, and being rational. Living like a stoic is being aware of yourself and striving to be in control of the escalation and emotional state of your thoughts.

Are you thinking you don't have time, or you are not ready to try a new way of thinking? There is a great e-newsletter you can subscribe to at www. ryanholiday.net. I also highly recommend kicking your day off with Ryan Holiday's book *The Daily Stoic: 366 Meditations on Wisdom, Perseverance, and the Art of Living* to get your mindset recalibrated for an amazing day. I feel good, connected, and happy when I read it. You can also start by focusing on just one of the four virtues below and build upon it as you get comfortable and form new habits.

The stoics value four cardinal virtues:

- Wisdom
- Justice
- Courage
- Moderation

Negative thoughts have been known to have serious consequences. The way we interpret the world around us is important to our mental and physical health because stress and negativity can have severe repercussions. By embracing the present moment and kicking our negative or overly self-aware thoughts to the curb, we can live a more positive and healthy life.

Exercise

1.   Which of the above virtues resonates most with you?

_____

_____

_____

_____

2.   Take some time in the morning or evening to speak kindly to yourself. Identify your biggest win from the day. What made you feel the happiest?

_____

_____

_____

_____

Chasing Manifestation

Have you ever believed in something so strongly that you could see the future unfolding before your eyes? Manifesting is a serious tool that has big results. Positive thinking and envisioning the future as though it has already happened is very powerful. The most successful people in the world positively visualize the future.

In 2012, Florida native Sara Blakely became the youngest female self-made billionaire due to her invention—Spanx. This brand of body-slimming women's apparel started with a $5,000 personal investment, a vision, and a commitment to a positive mindset. When she was sixteen, Blakely received Wayne Dyer's cassette tape series *How to Be a No Limit Person* as a parting gift from her dad before he left her and her mom. Through this gift, she learned that school teaches you what to think, not how to think, and this revelation helped her become incredibly successful at manifesting and knowing how to push forward despite whatever life threw at her.

Blakely sold fax machines door-to-door for seven years. Anyone who has done cold calling knows it is not an easy task. Her intuition and confidence served her well because she always pursued her need to change the world. She believes the masculine and feminine energy within us do not have to cancel each other out but can thrive in unity. She also believes business doesn't have to be cutthroat. In college, Blakely visualized herself on *Oprah*, and for the next decade, she continued to believe with 100 percent confidence it would be a reality—and eventually, it was!

When it is your calling and your vision, you must push yourself to make your why about something bigger than money or yourself. Blakely has done this. The investment firm Blackstone bought a majority stake in Spanx for an estimated $1.2 billion. Do you want to know how Blakely celebrated? She shared the wealth and gave her employees each two first-class plane tickets anywhere in the world and $10,000.

Blakely's why is promoting the future of women in business. She says her major driving force inspiration is the thought of her mom and grandma not having the opportunities she has had, so she took it upon herself to step up and take a swing on behalf of woman everywhere, especially those limited by forces beyond their control. Having a bigger why, a positive mindset, and trusting your gut is a recipe for empowering the soul!

Exercise

1. Is there something you really want? Visualize yourself having it. Write down what it is and the date you will receive it.

_____

_____

_____

_____

2. Describe a time when you went with your gut feeling. What was the result?

_____

_____

_____

_____

Summary

Some think the soul is separate from the body, that it is the spiritual part of humans, which is a beautiful and powerful thing. The soul isn't only empowered and nurtured through positive and fun events but by laughing, being resilient, not settling for mediocrity, and taking great care of your body and mind. Knowing how to silence your mind and still your body, and confidently being able to do so, will allow you to experience and nurture the energy inside you, thus allowing you to delight in peace and thrive in this crazy world.

CHAPTER 13
FEEDING THE ENTREPRENEURIAL SPIRIT

"I'm convinced that about half of what separates the successful entrepreneurs from the non-successful ones is pure perseverance."

— Steve Jobs

Now that we have had the chance to empower our souls, let's talk about feeding our entrepreneurial spirit. Entrepreneurship can sometimes be an insatiable hunger, something we can't quite fully understand unless we feed the entrepreneurial spirit. The secret sauce to being a successful entrepreneur is composed of four ingredients—fearlessness, a no-excuse attitude, giving more than you take and feeding off others' mistakes and triumphs. Read on to get cooking! In this chapter, I will include many examples of people, some now famous, who fed their entrepreneurial spirit and changed the world.

Creating a Sports Brand

My naive ego convinced me I would be guaranteed an awesome job in sports when I graduated. It didn't quite pan out, but let's start at the beginning. I was a senior in college and had my heart set on working in the NFL. Erin Andrews was the hot sportscaster at the time, and watching her on TV time and time again made me want to be just like her.

One day, I was scribbling company names and logos in my notebook during math class when I hit upon one I loved. This is how Sports Chat Fanatic (SCF) was born in my dorm at the University of New Haven. I began blogging about football and captured a niche fanbase. I got invited to talk about the Pittsburgh Steelers on a Tennessee radio station and got a press pass to attend the Walter Camp awards ceremony. I created a blog where I interviewed some NFL players, talked about my projections, and discussed the Pittsburgh Steelers' results. Unfortunately, no Steelers attended the Walter Camp awards that year, but I was still able to rub elbows with Harry Carson, Tony Dorsett, Leonard Marshall, and the All-American players of that year like Andrew Luck, whom I chatted with on the couch in the lobby of the Omni before he turned in for the night.

These were the days before Instagram, so I was on Facebook, Twitter, and YouTube. I was also a novice at using social media, so my strategy was not what it would be today. I have not taken down the content or videos I created because they remain a digital time capsule of my entrepreneurial journey. And boy, have I come a long way.

Creating a sports brand was a great time; I met a lot of people and watched a lot of football. However, as time went on, I knew deep down it wasn't my calling. I didn't want to do it forever, so I closed shop, finished up school, and entered the workforce.

More than ten years later, speaking with a former University of New Haven peer, we came up with the company Freestyle Football Club—a group of athletic entertainers—something like basketball freestylers, the Harlem Globetrotters. But this new company would feature soccer players, and we would be the premiere booking agency for all freestyler soccer performances at private and public events. I am laying some strategic partnerships and foundations now, but this is something that soccer fanatics can get really excited about. Providing a slice of soccer bliss at events will be the ultimate treat.

I am a firm believer in "slow and steady wins the race," not only because I'm slow as a Tortuga ("turtle"), but because this allows me to be prepared, be organized, and create a strong foundation. Also, Sports Chat Fanatic showed me that I can have an idea and make it happen. But I want to be able to create not just something fun for myself but an organization that

Photo Credit: Gregeiger Company Unlimited, Inc. (Leonard Marshall)

can give people the opportunity to live comfortably, take care of their families, work in a safe and accepting space, and provide the ultimate customer experience to brighten others' lives.

Sometimes, our ideas aren't the ones we want to stick with, but I have found the ones you are meant to do will never disappear from your mind.

Exercise

1. An angel investor believes in you and wants to invest in your big idea. What is your big idea?

    _____

    _____

    _____

2. Describe a job, idea, or hobby you once loved but outgrew. What did you replace it with?

    _____

    _____

    _____

Eating Fresh and Growing an Empire

Creating a future powerhouse business starts with an idea. It can be something as simple as dipped fruit or a submarine sandwich. Did you know Subway's journey started in Bridgeport, Connecticut? The iconic sub shop with its green and yellow logo revolutionized fast food by allowing you to watch the sandwich artists make the food while you watched. It is currently headquartered in my hometown of Milford, Connecticut.

Founder Fred Deluca began feeding his entrepreneurial spirit not with subs but by collecting empty soda bottles and redeeming them so he could buy comics. He then sold the comics and used the money to buy more.

However, his big idea played out five decades ago when a nuclear physicist named Dr. Peter Buck offered a college student some advice. He gave Fred DeLuca, who was struggling to pay for college, the idea of opening a submarine sandwich shop to help pay his tuition. Buck invested $1,000 and became DeLuca's mentor. DeLuca revolutionized the fast-food industry, and despite passing in 2015, his legacy will continue in the heart of the company and the world.

This venture changed the franchise world and gave the gift of entrepreneurship to thousands of franchise owners around the globe. DeLuca had no idea he would go on to create one of the top fast-food chains in the world.

Exercise

1. When selecting a brand, which core values are most important?

    _____

    _____

    _____

    _____

2. Which company's mission aligns best with your values?

    _____

    _____

    _____

    _____

Being an Entrepreneur

An entrepreneur is a person who creates, maintains, and operates a business or multiple businesses, and through the process, takes on risk. If the definition had an image, who would it be? For me, it would be Gary Vee. Gary Vaynerchuk is an immigrant from Belarus. He is known for being an author, speaker, and internet personality who contributes content abundantly to his community. He also has a great perspective on what it means to be an entrepreneur.

Either you are an entrepreneur or you are not because wanting to be an entrepreneur is like wanting to win the lottery. The odds are slim, and wanting it does nothing. Also, being an entrepreneur doesn't just magically happen. According to Gary Vee, "It's inherent in your personality, your aspirations, your goals, and sometimes, you can't control it." Also, having a full-time job is not entrepreneurship. Entrepreneurs can't survive within the constraints of a normal job.

Gary Vee has some tips for aspiring entrepreneurs:

1. Get a mentor(s).

2. Get work experience even if that means working for free under someone who can show you the ropes.

3. Learn to hustle and be willing to do whatever it takes to win.

4. Put yourself in a position to win by doing, not just reading or learning from a book.

Gary Vee adds: "If you want to be an artist, make art. Stop saying you want to do it and make the work happen. Want to open a pizza place? Great. Figure out exactly what you need to do and then start on those steps immediately."

When it comes down to it, true entrepreneurs are unstoppable; they thrive by and love hustling. If you aren't willing to do whatever it takes, then the life of an entrepreneur is most likely not for you, and that is okay. But if any of the above resonates with you, then get started—all it takes is one idea and the discipline to thrive.

Exercise

1. Are you an innovator or an executor?

    _____

    _____

    _____

    _____

2. Describe one thing you can do today to push your career forward, whether that is a normal job or an entrepreneurial venture.

    _____

    _____

    _____

    _____

Earning Potential

The start of high school caused me to make many adjustments. I had to adjust to a new school, new friends, a new curriculum, and new peer expectations. Many of my new friends and those I wanted to befriend had cell phones, so of course, I not only wanted one; I needed one. I made up my mind to ask my dad for one that first afternoon of high school. I remember standing outside of his office door pacing back and forth, scared to go in to ask because I knew it would take some convincing.

"Hey, Dad, I need to talk to you. Can I get a cell phone? The girls at school have them, and I really need one." My dad stared at me for a moment, then said, "Well, if you want one, you need to earn it. Get a job."

As the conversation continued, I became increasingly frustrated and entitled. Other girls' dads gave them their first cell phones on a silver platter. Where was mine? I was fuming and arguing with him, thinking he was crazy.

"Well, I can't get a job because I am not legally old enough to work." He calmly replied, "Well, if you can't get a job, then you can't get a phone." I complained, saying, "No one will hire me. This isn't fair." My dad said, "Well, if you want one that badly, you will find a way."

I left the conversation feeling frustrated and sad. However, I couldn't help thinking I would show him. I went upstairs to think, grabbing the Yellow Pages from the hall closet as I went. I was determined to get one of those cool flip razor phones as soon as I could. That was the popular model at the time, and I really wanted to start my high school career at Lauralton on a positive and trendy note. Who doesn't want to fit in at a private, Catholic, all-girl school, especially when one's mother insists upon her daughter wearing a frumpy, oversized uniform?

I leafed through my parents' big old yellow phone book until I reached the B section. I dragged my finger down the page until I reached Big Nonna's Cheer n' More. This was the little dance and cheerleading store we drove by every day on the way to school. I had been officially cheerleading for six, going on seven years, so I had the cheering experience but not the business or work experience. I knew I was up for working and would do what I had to do so I could prove myself. Especially if it meant getting my cell phone.

After three rings, a woman answered. "Hello, Big Nonna's Cheer n' More."

"Hi. I am not sure if you are hiring, but I am a cheerleader, and I would love to work at your shop to help with whatever you need."

After a brief pause, the woman, who was named Coreen DeMayo, asked if I wanted to come in the next day. Boom Shakalaka! I was quite pleased with myself. Shortly after my dad had challenged me to earn a cell phone by getting a job, I had. However, I also did not want my dad to know he was right, and that I could, in fact, get a job at my age. I decided not to tell my dad right away.

I accumulated a nice chunk of money making $6.00 an hour. I was delighted to be working in a cheerleading store and helping other cheerleaders and dancers get sized for shoes, uniforms, jackets, etc. I took great joy in meeting new people and learning about business and how a small boutique functions. I learned client service techniques and how to send in purchase orders, invoice coaches, and pay bills. I did so well at the shop that DeMayo occasionally ran errands, leaving me in charge of the store. Her trust made me feel accomplished.

While I was saving up for my phone, my dad learned I had landed a part-time job up the street. Not the type of person to make a big deal out of things, he acknowledged the accomplishment in an encouraging way and reminded me that when I had the money, he would take me to pick out my phone. Working a few days a week for a few hours, I soon had enough money to buy my phone! I counted the crisp dollars and walked into my dad's office.

"Hey, Dad, I have the money to buy my phone."

He swiveled around in his executive chair and smiled. "All right, let's go to Verizon and pick out your phone."

My dad is a man of his word, and on that day, he stayed true to his promise. If I earned the money and brought it to him, he would drop what he was doing and bring me to Verizon.

Just because you have something doesn't mean you earned it, and just because you want something doesn't mean you deserve it. I am glad my dad didn't cave and give me an unearned cell phone. The phone meant so much to me, and I appreciated it because I wasn't entitled to it. This lesson has stuck with me, inspiring my work ethic and appreciation for what I have and proving to me that if there is a will, there is a way; all you have to do is set a goal, make the first move toward what you want, and be resilient

Exercise

1. What is the greatest lesson you learned from your childhood?

_____

_____

_____

_____

2. Whether you have children now or want them in the future, what les-
    son(s) do you want to instill in them?

    _____

    _____

    _____

    _____

Leaving a Legacy of Lemons

What is the best frozen lemonade in the world? If you don't know what
Del's is, you probably don't live in Rhode Island and are missing out on
some of the best frozen lemonade out there.

Del's started with a man fondly known as Great-Grandfather DeLucia. He
lived in Naples, Italy, and made the first Del's Frozen Lemonade back in
1840. He made the refreshing drink by placing snow into local caves during
winter and insulating it with straw. Then in summer, he used ripe local
lemons and mixed their juice with sugar and snow. He sold this concoction
at the local market, and it was quite the hit, especially since fruit ices are
popular in Europe.

Franco DeLucia brought his father's frozen lemonade recipe to America at
the turn of the twentieth century. Angelo DeLucia, Franco DeLucia's son,
began work on a machine to produce the frozen lemonade and a meth-
od for making it a consistently excellent product. In 1948, Del's Frozen
Lemonade was born and became the sole product sold at the little, fami-

ly-owned stand in Cranston, Rhode Island. Soon, Angelo designed the first units capable of being sent to and served anywhere in the state.

When Angelo's son Bruce entered the family business, they had five franchises in Rhode Island. Since then, Bruce has helped the business flourish and grow. Now, there are Del's franchises worldwide providing the refreshing, all-natural treat to everyone, anywhere.

Bruce's daughter, Stephanie, is now in the family business. She is president of Del's Lemonade's sister company, Francesca Enterprises International. Stephanie also works directly with web sales, promotions, and marketing. This Italian family continues growing their lemon legacy, and it is worth a taste if you ever visit Rhode Island.

Exercise

1. If you started a family business, what would it be?

   _____

   _____

   _____

2. What do you hope to pass down to your family when you retire?

   _____

   _____

   _____

Surfing to Success

All it takes is an idea, and sometimes that idea starts with couch surfing. If you don't know what couch surfing is, you have never had to temporarily stay in an improvised sleeping arrangement.

If you like to travel, you probably have heard of Airbnb. This brilliant tech business started with a simple idea and revolutionized travel accommodations, giving people all over the world the gift of supplemental income.

Brian Chesky, the founder of Airbnb, was a former hockey player and industrial design major. Chesky attended the Rhode Island School of Design (RISD) where he met his longtime friend and co-founder Joe Gebbia. Flashback to the days leading up to graduation when Gebbia reportedly said, "There's something I need to tell you. We're going to start a company one day, and they're going to write a book about it."

In 2007, Chesky and Gebbia decided to rent out their apartment during a design conference. Since hotels were booked, accommodations were in demand even if it was a non-conventional stay on an air mattress with a continental breakfast consisting of Pop Tarts. They launched Airbedandbreakfast.com in 2008, which became Airbnb. Joe's visualizing and their collective ingenuity helped them make a huge mark on the travel industry. Today, Airbnb has listings in more than 191 countries and is one of the most valuable startups in history, valued at $18 billion, proving it pays to couch surf and travel.

Exercise

1. Describe the best accommodations you have ever had.

    _____

    _____

    _____

    _____

2. If you could stay at an Airbnb anywhere in the world, where would you stay?

    _____

    _____

    _____

    _____

Moving in a New Direction

Have you ever felt compelled to follow your heart? Have you felt the sensation of the Universe, God, or some Higher Power beckoning you down a special path, and when you step foot on the path, it lights up with each step?

I will always love music. I started college as a music management major. Throughout my junior and senior years of high school, I trained to get into music school to become a musical therapist so I could help people with Alzheimer's and sensory issues to heal through music. I thought this was what I was supposed to do, but all the colleges for this niche major were three or more hours away, and when my dad got sick in 2006, I knew I couldn't go far from my family. I also didn't get into the highly competitive music therapy programs at the University of Miami, Temple University, or the Berklee College of Music. I know now this wasn't an accident. I wasn't supposed to be a music therapist.

I decided to go to Manhattanville College in Purchase, New York, for their music entertainment degree. It didn't take long before being graded on my musical talent became a burden. Practicing became a chore, and I started losing interest. Simultaneously, another path lit up when I took two core classes, a Marketing 101 course and an Intro to Law class, that sparked a fire of excitement in me I didn't know existed. We had a project that was so fun it felt like I was playing a boardgame.

We had to invent a product. I came up with the idea of a suit for infants that covered their whole body so that when they ate, their clothes wouldn't get soiled. Think of it as a full body bib. It was made from eco-friendly, reusable materials that allowed the parent to simply throw it in the dishwasher. At the time, I didn't know that sustainability and the baby market boom would end up being a money maker and trend. Looking back, I really wish I had pursued this invention.

Here is my note of encouragement to you: If you have an idea, even if it seems like it is too simple or commonsensical, and it doesn't exist, pursue it. Had I taken that product to market, I would have achieved my entrepreneurial success earlier.

At Manhattanville College, I also took a pre-law class where I fell in love with legal procedures and the ability to lean upon previous rulings to try to make a case. I loved that both marketing and law had the ability to speculate and draw new conclusions in contrast to science and math where the answer is the answer. I was and still am all about the gray areas and the possibilities of not having one way to interpret or execute something. Hindsight is always 20/20. I went on to switch majors when I transferred to the University of New Haven and became a marketing major with a paralegal minor. The switch set me up for entrepreneurial and business success.

Otraway didn't start off as a marketing agency. It began in 2017 after my return from Argentina where I found my biological family. I came back with a sense of awareness of myself and others. I committed to doing more to help people and make a difference in the lives of other adoptees. I had an idea for helping adoptees discover their roots by facilitating trips to Paraguay. I wanted eventually to expand to other countries to reunite other adoptees like me with their families.

I wanted a company name that didn't exist and was not obviously identified without understanding the story—which, for a marketer, doesn't exactly make sense, but it is what I felt compelled to do. I combined Spanish and English words into a hybrid word, "Otraway," which means "another way" because I planned to do things differently with my business to truly have a community focus and better the world. I helped create a prominent icon that resembled a compass and direction to symbolize not only my connection to the north and south of the western hemisphere but my journey from south to north.

I worked with a few people, helping them with their journey to Paraguay. And when I couldn't help with their trip or the person wasn't ready for the journey to their past, I listened and gave advice on coping with their life, resentment, sadness, and more.

As time went on, the program and pricing just didn't feel right. I couldn't charge people for something I felt they had a right to know and do. Also, Stroessner's dictatorship and the adoption issues that occurred after his reign caused so much pain and corruption, I didn't feel right profiting from it.

Not every adoptee had the beautiful upbringing or happy closure I had experienced, so I also didn't have the mental capacity to take on many other people's emotions and hardship when I was still processing my own adoption story. I could have created a nonprofit, but the red tape and restrictions on nonprofits were daunting. I knew that owning a for profit company and running it on my terms would allow me to give more back and help adoptees down the road—or even fund an orphanage. I opted for patience, taking my time to figure out what my illuminated path had in store for me.

In 2018, my first son, Luca, was born and so was my revamped vision for Otraway. I refreshed the logo and shaped my mission to help business owners and entrepreneurs succeed while giving back a portion of their profits to the community. I took a hands-on community marketing approach and encouraged my clients to include philanthropy in their business plans. In 2019, I only did okay because I was focused on raising Luca and strategically getting my ducks in a row. My first true year in business was 2020, the year I moved to Rhode Island. Despite the many uncertainties of 2020, and not having a business network in the state, I was able to make just shy of $100,000 in revenue. I learned a lot that year about wasted time, giving more than I have, not having a conservative budget, and spending money on things that didn't end up serving the bigger picture.

Aside from the giving back, one of the biggest entrepreneurial lessons I have learned is always to say thank you and show gratitude. This is something my dad taught me. Whenever I interview for a job, I make it a point to send a thank you letter overnight because a thank you carries so much weight. People understand time is priceless and special, so if someone takes time to sit down with you, you should always be grateful. When someone takes moments from their fleeting life to give to you, respect it.

The other major lesson I learned is about patience, which is important in parenting and, really, anything you do. The best enterprises shouldn't come easily, and sometimes the most successful ventures, ideas, and projects are the ones that take the most preparation and patience. A lesson learned is valuable and can be shared, so please learn from my mistakes and tribulations so you can be better and more successful than me.

My entrepreneurial journey has been a series of winding paths, dead ends, and most importantly, lights. I am human, so I have veered off the path many times and been distracted by false trails, but I keep coming back to the same core values, gifts, goals, and dreams. I also accept that I will always be an entrepreneur taking risks, pursuing ideas that sometimes seem a bit crazy, and hustling to make things happen.

Exercise

1. Describe a time when you started a project that morphed into some-
    thing better.

    _____

    _____

    _____

    _____

2. Do you typically approach things in a fast and aggressive way or cau-
    tious and steady? Have there been times when you should have used
    the opposite approach?

    _____

    _____

    _____

    _____

Summary

Sometimes you will feel like you are on top of the world, and sometimes you
will feel like a failure. The highs and lows of entrepreneurship can sometimes feel manic, but if you can work through the hardships, the mistakes,
the rejections, and the people closest to you thinking you're nuts, and cling
to the discipline to sort through the endless abyss of ideas and thoughts,
you will make big things happen for yourself and others. By focusing on

what matters, like passion, patience, efficiency, and authenticity, you will find success and learn to snap back into focus when you get distracted.

CHAPTER 14
CHASING YOUR DREAMS

"At the end of the day, it's not about what you have or even what you've accomplished. It's about who you've lifted up and who you've made better. It's about what you've given back."

— Denzel Washington

In the last chapter, we talked about feeding the entrepreneurial spirit. Now we will explore chasing your dreams. Dreams can be vastly different, depending on who you are, where you are, and what stage of life you are in. It is important to have dreams, and it is also important to reassess your dreams at different stages in your life because we all evolve over time.

Chasing the Past

Have you heard the phrase, "The apple doesn't fall far from the tree"? This common saying makes sense, but what if your tree is an undefined species?

I went with Peter, my then-boyfriend, to his futsal game (a form of football/soccer played on a hard court with a small soccer-like ball), and while I was watching, I saw his friend's father who runs the league. I had never met him before, but I instantly recognized him because he looked very similar to his son. When I looked at Pete's father sitting beside me, I noticed he and Peter look very much alike as well. Their features and build are linked by one thing—their DNA. Being adopted, the phenomena of DNA has always been a mystery to me. Before I went to Paraguay, I couldn't help but wonder how I would compare if I stood beside my birth parents or relatives. Would our black hair look the same? Would we have the same noses and almond eyes? Did I have siblings who looked like me? The questions that regularly ran through my mind were endless.

Before I met my biological family in 2015, I was often chasing the past.

In 2006, California-based 23andMe was founded as a personal genomics and biotech company. It provides consumers a safe place to explore and comprehend their own genes by providing access to a gene database and easy-to-digest results, which have been life-changing for many people. The company was founded by Anne Wojcicki.

Being adopted, I badly wanted to connect some dots to my past to help me feel more grounded in the present. I opted for purchasing the 23andMe genetic test to help put together some more pieces of my puzzle. The results I got were amazing. I have 906 third and fourth cousins, which makes sense since when I traveled to Paraguay, I found out I have five younger siblings and nine aunts and uncles. Therefore, saying I am biologically from a huge family is an understatement. I only wish I could locate some first and second cousins, but based on the poverty and challenges in South America, I am not surprised there were few relatives on 23andMe. Despite not being connected to them, knowing I have many first cousins excites me, and I feel closer to finding out more about my past and biological family. My possible birth father reached out while Pete and I were gone on our honeymoon. Before I turn thirty-five, I have decided to do a DNA test to see if he is, in fact, my biological father. It has taken me some time before I have been ready to unveil another mystery. Until then, my past will be a mystery to some extent, and I am finally at peace with this fact.

Exercise

1. Have you tried a service like 23andMe? What happened? If not, what are your reservations?

   _____

   _____

   _____

   _____

   _____

2. If you could solve any mystery in the world, what would it be?

   _____

   _____

   _____

   _____

   _____

Chasing Stuff

I had the opportunity to attend a ribbon cutting for an expansion at Sheehan High School while on the Board of Education. It was very exciting to be a part of a ceremony that celebrates growth and educational opportunities for young people. Since I was on the Board of Education, each of the nine board members would take turns attending events and speaking on behalf of the board. I went to the ceremony straight from work, and because I got stuck in traffic, I had some time to prepare my short speech. One of my biggest pet peeves is forgetting to make a point or not saying something I should, but I give this little speech a thumbs-up because, overall, I got my points across.

After the ceremony, I was chatting with Justin Marciano, the assistant principal and my former college English professor, about traveling. He had been to Italy, so I explained that my husband Peter and I were going backpacking through Italy for our honeymoon. Justin immediately started telling me about his trip to Italy and all the spots to visit.

Side note: Before we knew each other, Peter and I had both transferred to the University of New Haven in our sophomore years. As I mentioned earlier, we met in Justin Marciano's English class, and the rest is history. I find it interesting that, while writing this book, I have found more and more instances of crossing paths with the same people repeatedly. I don't take this lightly, and I know these encounters happen at pivotal points where I had an opportunity to learn some awesome lessons that helped shape the trajectory of my life.

Justin and I agreed that travel and stepping out of one's comfort zone are huge benefits for everyone, especially young people. Being immersed in another country's culture, food, and history is such a fruitful and valuable experience.

While I was there, Justin was talking with a student about buying some shiny, expensive rims for the student's car. Justin told the student when he was younger, he looked at a picture of the Coliseum in Rome and thought it was the coolest thing since sliced bread. At that moment, high-school age Justin made the conscious decision to do whatever it took to go see it in person. He saved up money and was able to visit Italy as a teenager—he accomplished his goal.

The student asked, "Why would you save your money for that?"

"In twenty years, you won't remember the rims you bought for your car, but you would remember a cool trip to Italy," Justin said.

I could see the wanderlust in Justin's eyes as he spoke and relived the memories. I could also tell he truly remembers his experience in Italy as a high school student. Material possessions tend not to end up being priceless memories like travel does. The student replied, "Wow, I never thought of it like that!" That is why we need educators like Justin to work with our young people—to engage and inspire them.

Justin's wisdom inspired me to pass up the next tempting fancy coffee purchase because I sure as hell won't remember a skinny latte next week, much less next year, but I will forever remember an amazing honeymoon and excursion to new places with my family—these are the experiences I live for and now save my money for.

Exercise

1. Describe a time when you purchased something expensive and it just ended up collecting dust?

    _____

    _____

    _____

    _____

2. What is the most memorable experience you have had or the most memorable place you have traveled to?

    _____

    _____

    _____

    _____

3. What unnecessary thing do you purchase regularly that you could eliminate so you can save the money for a trip?

    _____

    _____

    _____

    _____

Chasing a Mission

Do you know any first responders or veterans? Have you ever thanked them for their service? Lord knows it takes a courageous and strong individual to dedicate their life to potentially deadly and PTSD-inducing work. The work and sacrifice of these brave folks is amazing and should be appreciated and respected.

When I think of chasing freedom and safety, I think of the brave men and women who enlist in the six branches of the United States military: Army, Navy, Air Force, Coast Guard, Marine Corps, and Space Force. Regardless of which democratic country you live in, the fight to create and preserve democracy, freedom, and civilian safety is very important.

Karen Dalton at the Dare to Dream Ranch is a woman in Rhode Island dedicated to shedding light on the challenges veterans face. She has devoted her life to helping veterans deal with issues associated with trauma or traumatic events and ensuring they get the tools and resources to cope with their stress. Dare to Dream Ranch is an alternative military retreat for past and present service members and their families. The ranch provides holistic programming designed to help their clients cope with and overcome PTSD, anxiety, depression, military sexual trauma, and mild traumatic brain injuries through healing, discovering their passion, and learning to become successful civilians. They offer programs such as: equine therapy, yoga, massage, horticulture, beekeeping, group therapy, nutrition, healthy cooking, fly fishing, and much more.

This cause is near and dear to me, and I will continue volunteering my time and shedding light on these heroic individuals and the organizations that exist to serve the needs of veterans and first responders. Did you know that many first responders are also veterans? Nineteen percent of police officers are veterans, and the military is the third most common career for vets according to a report based on US Census data by Gregory B. Lewis and Rahul Pathak of Georgia State University for The Marshall Project. Many people who were in foster care also go into the military.

Veterans and first responders make local communities better all over, and it is not an easy job. I will always treasure the sacrifices of people like my grandfather and brother for keeping the peace and protecting our freedoms and the opportunities we have today in the United States. I regularly remind myself that I could still be living in South America struggling, but I'm blessed to be in the United States. So many people will never get the chance to be here. I will never lose sight of this fact, nor my respect for these amazing men and women. Next time you see someone rocking a veteran cap or an active duty uniform or you see "veteran" on a license plate, say "Hello" and "Thank you."

Exercise

1. Describe a time when you or someone you know needed a first responder?

_____

_____

_____

2. Have you ever helped someone in need? How did you feel?

_____

_____

_____

_____

Chasing Love

Do you fall head over heels in love fast like me? Are you a hopeless roman-tic hoping to find the one? I began dating my husband Peter when I was eighteen. As I mentioned before, we met in our English literature class. I thought the older guy with the crisp, white, fitted hat and white Reebok sneakers was cute, so I passed him a note asking him out. We went out that evening to a little dive bar called Marc Anthony's on Campbell Ave in West Haven, Connecticut. We hit it off and have been close ever since.

In 2009, a year after we started dating, Pete thought it would be a good idea to take the chicken wing bones from our dinner, dry them out, skewer them, and string them together so he could wear them as a necklace as part of his Halloween costume. I was repulsed by this idea, but he is stubborn, and when he decides on something, that is it. His goal was to be a freaky voodoo shaman for Halloween, and who was I to rain on his creative parade?

Pete's costume was makeshift and consisted of black attire from head to toe with a random, creepy chicken bone necklace. It said witch doctor to no one except the two of us. It was the opposite of sexy, and I'll admit it is better we were already dating because this costume was a bit bizarre. It certainly wouldn't have won him any brownie points in the love department.

We went to a party, and an hour or two into it, Pete was more wasted than a frat boy at a St. Paddy's Day parade—thanks Jägermeister. The smell of licorice (Jägermeister smells like black licorice) was oozing out of his pores, which nearly made me gag. Blah! We escaped upstairs to an air mattress to get away from the party. I was hoping for some hanky-panky time, but he was past the point of making any worthwhile moves, and for the record, I hate licorice. We sat down and he began to babble about "In ten years…."

He kept saying, "You know, in ten years…." He kept asking me if I knew what would happen in ten years. I quizzically looked at him and wondered if the alcohol had triggered some psychotic break. It was early in our relationship, and I was his first serious girlfriend, so the concept of a decade from then kind of freaked me out. At the time, I didn't even know what I wanted to major in, let alone what my relationship status would be in ten years.

During those mysterious ten years that he brought up at that Halloween party, so much has happened. We have a couch that no longer embarrasses us when company comes over. Our old couch looked nice from afar, but the unlucky person who sat on the left side would basically be sitting on the floor. Still, we think back on our first furniture fondly.

Now we have a dresser with a mirror attached, so we are high rollers. Our home finally looks like someone lives there, and it's no longer a mismatched mess.

It can be quite frustrating to rent or own your own place, as can living with another person, whether it is a roommate, spouse, or significant other. Things like money, groceries, sharing, cleaning, and important decisions suddenly become controversial because two minds are coming together from two different sets of experiences.

Over the years Pete and I have lived together, we have made some hysterical memories. For example, putting the bread in the fridge. I was really tired one morning, and I had kept asking Pete to stop putting the bread in the fridge because, growing up, my family left it on the counter. In my sleepy, barely awake state of mind, I sent him the following text: "If you put the bread in the fridge one more time, I will cut you." We still look back at this and laugh—in case you were wondering, we keep the bread in the fridge now, and I am okay with it.

Before we got our first real mattress, we slept on an air mattress. Every morning, Pete would get up first to get ready for work. When he got off the air mattress, I would sink to the floor with a thud. It was so annoying, but these are the memories that are saved as a time capsule in my mind of where we started. Moving from our air mattress to an ecofriendly, comfy mattress was life-changing and showed me truly how far we have come.

We have had our share of memorable, funny, and not-so-funny moments. We value the experiences and love looking back to see how far we have come. When we are in Connecticut, we make a point of driving by our old apartment and reflecting on the good old, yet sometimes frustrating days. It is crazy to think maybe those gross chicken bones had some sort of power or maybe Pete manifested good things for us with his ten years from now talk. I will probably never know what he was really trying to say, but I am grateful.

And something amazing did happen around ten years later. I gave birth to my rainbow baby Luca and found the greatest love of my life when I became a mom.

I had Luca after having a miscarriage, and the year after his birth was one of the most emotionally challenging of my life. I survived and realized I am unstoppable and stronger than I ever imagined. Every time I am having challenges, I take one look at my sons and the love I feel for them and find the hope and joy to get through anything.

Exercise

1. Share some aspect of your life today that seems to be or is the result of an idea or dream you had long ago.

   _____

   _____

   _____

   _____

2. Describe the best/worst party/event you ever attended. What specifically made it memorable?

_____

_____

_____

_____

Chasing Culture

Have you ever had a strong passion that led you to pursue a journey to another country? Immersion in other cultures can be among the most rewarding and educational experiences. Such experiences not only teach us things about other people but ourselves. They can also affect our life path.

Patricia Doerr, whom I fondly refer to as Mom, fell in love with Spanish language and culture in ways she never imagined possible. Her passion led her to the Yucatan Peninsula region of México in 1972. She participated in a summer work-study program that was sponsored by the Catholic Church. This program was affiliated with six colleges and universities in the northwest region of Pennsylvania. Patricia was attending Edinboro University and was joined by eight fellow students.

The program provided Patricia with an opportunity to experience two diverse cultural settings—life in the capital of the Yucatan and in a primitive village called Tizimin. During this five-week adventure, the students spent the weekends in Mérida, where they attended seminars on various aspects

of Mayan civilization and visited Mayan ruins on the peninsula. All participants arranged their own transportation to México and paid a $15 room
and board fee. They were shepherded around by a missionary couple, who
were their contacts throughout the trip.

Patricia enjoyed the seminars and visiting the sites, but what she found
most rewarding was getting to know the people. While in Mérida, the group
stayed in a rustic motel-like building that served as a retreat for seminary
students. They slept in handmade hammocks to avoid cuddling with the
hairy tarantulas and scorpions that took refuge in their rooms from time
to time. Scorpions were drawn to damp, moist areas so they regularly had
to inspect the shower stalls before showering. One evening while they were
sitting and chatting in one room, a very large tarantula crawled up the wall!

The students were divided into four groups of two, and on Monday mornings, they were sent to four different primitive towns to perform community service. The priest in each village assigned the community service.
Patricia and another student, Mary Beth, were assigned to an orphanage
for girls under twelve called La Casa de Cristianidad. Each day they sang,
danced, and spoke Spanish with these wonderful little girls.

The girls were excited and fascinated by the light-skinned Americans, Patricia and Mary Beth. The girls rarely left the orphanage, which was sur-
rounded by a high stone wall. Many of the children did not know how old
they were because the nuns would often find children who had been aban-
doned outside the large wooden doors of the orphanage. What bothered
Patricia beyond words was that these precious little girls could only stay at
the orphanage until they were twelve because new children were always ap-

pearing on the doorstep. They would then be assigned to wealthy families to be cooks and housekeepers.

While in Tizimin, Mary Beth and Patricia lived with a wonderful family, consisting of a mother, father, and three children. The family was middle to upper class because they had a cook and housekeeper. The family didn't talk to the housekeeper and discouraged socializing because she was from a lower social class and considered to be help, not part of the family.

Patricia saw the young girl as one of the sweet girls in the orphanage. At one point, this young girl had not been an indentured servant living in isolation. She may even have played innocently with friends within the orphanage's walls. The girl's plight affected Patricia so greatly she tried to convince her mother to adopt a child from the orphanage. Of course, that was impossible because two years before the trip to Mexico, Patricia's father, Clinton Stevenson, had abruptly died of cancer at age forty. Her mother, Helen Stevenson, was a young widow with four children younger than Patricia to care for, surviving solely on Social Security and some financial support from in-laws.

Patricia made a promise to herself that one day she would adopt a child because she had seen firsthand how many children in the world needed parents. When she married Daniel Doerr, she tried to convince him to adopt, but he wanted to have a couple of children of their own first.

For years, Patricia clipped articles featuring parents adopting children from around the world. I'm not sure my mom realized it then, but she was manifesting something big for her family. The trip to Mexico deeply affected her life journey, helped her heal after she lost her father, and introduced the idea of adopting a Hispanic daughter. After giving birth to two sons, she was finally able to convince Daniel to begin looking into a foreign adoption. Sixteen years after her trip to Mexico, they were able to adopt me from Paraguay.

Exercise

1. What has been your biggest lesson learned while traveling?

    _____

    _____

    _____

    _____

2. Describe a time when you felt compelled to change your life.

    _____

    _____

    _____

    _____

Finding the Best Talent

Have you ever heard someone lament, "Good help is hard to find"? Finding the right fit for a position to push a company forward can be challenging.

Hiring the wrong person can be catastrophic to your business while finding a rockstar employee can help drive your success. What is the secret to hiring? Think outside the box.

The CEO of Charles Schwab, Walt Bettinger, has a unique way of interviewing prospects. He asks open-ended questions and looks for responses that reflect the person's ability to take responsibility and react in a favorable manner. He also has a character test he gives to get a feel for the person. Bettinger will take the individual out for a meal and ensure the interviewee's order gets messed up. Life is full of things that don't go to plan, so Bettinger's goal is to test the candidate's demeanor and reaction when something goes wrong to get a better understanding of how the person would deal with adversity. Bettinger knows kindness and composure go a long way in business and life. He also watches to see if the person ignores the issue, which would indicate the person was too passive to say anything. It may also indicate that the person doesn't pay attention to detail or is too shy to make a correction.

"We're all going to make mistakes," Bettinger concludes. "The question is how are we going to recover when we make them, and are we going to be respectful to others when they make them?"

Exercise

1. What qualities would your ideal employee possess?

   _____

   _____

2. Describe a cringeworthy customer experience you witnessed. What went wrong?

_____

_____

_____

_____

3. How do you react when something gets messed up or you experience poor communication or service?

_____

_____

_____

_____

Searching for Connections

Throughout my career, I was chasing the wrong thing and ignoring my calling. Recently, though, I learned my years of networking have paid off in a profound way. Not only have I been able to discover the many different professions and opportunities that exist, but I have also met thousands of people from different walks of life. I learned about culture, traditions, love, and life. Learning the importance of networking and being kind when you are still young is worth its weight in gold. Here are some ways you can take advantage of learning about networking in various areas of your life:

- **School:** In high school and college, you will have so many opportunities to connect and learn from your peers. Besides making connections in classes, you can join a variety of different groups to meet people with similar interests and goals. I also picked up a minor in law, which equated to the same number of credits needed to get a paralegal certificate. If you have already graduated, tapping into your alumni network is another opportunity. You can also pick up certificates and use LinkedIn's education portal or request to shadow or intern in an area of interest.

- **Referral Networking:** A referral networking group can be great. I have been part of Business Network International (BNI) for several years, and it has consistently generated 50 percent of my company's revenue. If you are new to a state or need a little public speaking experience, you have the perfect opportunity to get to know a core group of people, learn about other businesses, and grow whatever your own project may be. Tread lightly with giving unqualified referrals, though, because when you refer someone, you put your reputation on the line. The Giver's Gain mentality is why my business has grown!

- **Extracurriculars:** Don't be afraid to treat life like college. Be curious, join activities and groups, and be open to new people and experiences. Join a Toastmasters, Rotary International, or Civics club; volunteer and apply for a Board of Directors position or whatever piques your interest. Once you join and become a member, introduce yourself, meet new people, and be confident. As time has gone on, I have become more and more capable of being unafraid to join a group even if I know no one in it, and I introduce myself regardless of whom I meet—a CEO, celebrity, someone I admire—they all wake up and put on their pants just like me. If you think of it in that light, you will not be afraid of someone's power, fame, or fortune because people are still people. So, go be you, and most importantly, have fun!

Networking isn't magic, but nor is it something to take lightly. Nurturing relationships is important and should be approached authentically. It can take seven or more interactions before you do business with someone, so be patient, kind, and have fun fostering long-term, meaningful connections. When you do this, good will come.

Exercise

- Describe a time when your network had a positive effect on your life.

_____

_____

_____

- List five people who were big connectors in your life. If you haven't spoken to them in a while, reach out, check in, and say thank you.

_____

_____

_____

_____

Jamming Through Life as a Ganador

Something I personally love about music is that it is a series of tones, rhythms, poetic words, and beats that evoke a very deep connection and bring people together.

Nick Rivera Caminero, also known as Nicky Jam, is a Puerto Rican and Dominican musician born in Boston. He has been blessed with the gift of music and drive. When he was a boy, his family moved to Cataño, Puerto Rico, and when he was twelve, he worked in a grocery store to make money to help pay for bread and contribute to his family's finances. His biggest musical influences were Al Green, LL Cool J, Run DMC, and of course, Michael Jackson. When he was eight, Caminero saw Michael Jackson's "Thriller" video and immediately knew he wanted to be a musician and performer.

In the mid-1990s, Nicky joined forces with Puerto Rican rapper Daddy Yankee. Later, in 2001, they collaborated, and one of Nicky's songs, "Tu Cuerpo En La Cama," was included on Yankee's *Cartel III* album. Unfortunately, Nicky's struggle with drugs broke up the duo. Nicky had battled addiction before and would again. His past was dark and ridden with hardship since both his parents also struggled with drug addiction. Nicky ended up in jail for three years before he decided to stop living in darkness and committed to breaking the cycle. Through discipline, faith in God, and the desire to create a better future for his family, he was able to push through to a better life.

Nicky's failure showed him what life is like on the bottom, and his success has showed him what it's like to be a *ganador* (a winner). It is much better being on top.

Discipline can give you a beautiful career, stability, and a leg up against other talented folks. Faith in God motivated Nicky and gave him the mental clarity to do things right and be successful. His faith showed him life is bigger than just him.

Exercise

1. List three scenarios in which you feel like your true self?

    _____

    _____

    _____

    _____

    _____

2. What are your three biggest motivators?

    _____

    _____

    _____

    _____

    _____

Summary

Everyone is motivated by something, whether it is money, notoriety, dreams, acknowledgment, serving others, relationships, or something else. Most people are motivated by a combination of things and circumstances. Regardless of the dream or goal you are chasing, always remember to have a why bigger than yourself and send the elevator down for others so they, too, can achieve their wildest dreams.

CHAPTER 15
CHALLENGING THE STATUS QUO

"I'm not interested in preserving the status quo; I want to overthrow it."

— Niccolo Machiavelli

I n the last chapter, we talked about chasing dreams. Now we will talk about shattering the glass ceiling and challenging the status quo. Throughout history, individuals have stepped up and challenged the system, the status quo, and the norms. Their courage enabled them to speak out, stand up, and change the future.

Keeping Up the Tempo

The Queen of Soul is not someone who lets adversity get in her way. Despite losing her mother when she was ten, having babies at twelve and fourteen, and struggling with alcoholism in her family, Aretha Franklin kept moving forward.

Franklin's passion for music came naturally. She grew up in a musical family. After her first son was born, she dropped out of school and began traveling with her father's gospel group. This experience made her grow up fast.

In 1956, when Franklin was still a teenager, she signed with the J.V.B. record label, which released her first single "Never Grow Old" that year. Later, in 1960, she signed with Columbia Records, but her career didn't hit its climax until she signed with Atlantic Records in 1966. Atlantic's Jerry Wexler was able to cultivate Franklin's talent and repurpose the sorrow she kept locked away in her soul. Her hit song "Respect" became an anthem for various fights for equality and respect all over.

Franklin's career covered five decades. In that time, she had 100 singles on the Billboard charts, received a total of eighteen Grammys, and sang at three presidential inaugurations. She was the first woman inducted into the Rock and Roll Hall of Fame.

Dominating the music charts wasn't Franklin's only calling. She was a civil rights activist and advocate for women's and Native American rights. She traveled with Martin Luther King, Jr. and received a special award for her dedication to civil rights from the Southern Christian Leadership Conference.

Franklin said, "Being the queen is not all about singing, and being a diva is not all about singing. It has much to do with your service to people. And your social contributions to your community and your civic contributions as well."

Aretha Franklin passed away on August 6, 2018; however, her music and legacy as the queen of soul will remain. Franklin is an example of how childhood tragedy and trauma do not have to destroy the gift we have to share with the world. Sometimes pain can have a silver lining, but not everyone will turn that pain into beautiful melodic art.

Exercise

1. If you had to pick your personal anthem, which song would it be?

    _____

    _____

    _____

    _____

    _____

2. Which painful moment in your childhood inspired you?

    _____

    _____

    _____

    _____

    _____

Taking a Stand

The desire to help others has always been at the core of my being, but my journey to my past and finding my birth family really brought about a sense of purpose and philanthropy. I am at peace with my past and accept that I am here for a reason. I didn't get to the United States by chance. It was fate, and my destiny is to share my story and inspire people through my words, experiences, love, and respect for life.

When I got back from South America, I was on a mission to make a difference in a larger number of people's lives. While abroad, I witnessed what my life could have been had I not been adopted. I witnessed extreme poverty and learned about the rampant corruption that is still happening today. This inspired me to step out of my comfort zone and try something new that would allow me to give back to my community in a big way. Destiny has a way of spotlighting our next steps.

I asked my mentor and colleague on the Board of the Spanish Community of Wallingford (SCOW) Steve Knight how I could become more involved in the community. I said the trip really inspired me and made me realize I am not doing enough for others. Knight suggested I consider running for the open Republican Board of Education seat in the upcoming election. Two Republican members were running for town council seats, so theoretically, two seats were open.

I toyed with the idea of running for about a week or two. I considered the time commitment and called to learn about the experience of current BOE members.

Then I took the political plunge. I had about three months to campaign. I went door to door, waved signs, handed out branded items with my name at the Celebrate Wallingford Festival, and met as many people as possible. I was at a slight disadvantage—in hindsight that was the self-doubt and limiting beliefs getting into my head—because I didn't grow up in Wallingford, had no street credibility, and no political experience (unless you count my brief stint as Lieutenant Governor of the Connecticut YMCA Youth and Government program). What I did have was grit, marketing, and branding expertise, and a hardcore belief that if there is a will, there's a way. Time and time again, I have seen my hard work and the hard work of others pay off.

The afternoon of the election, I invited Angel, the ten-year-old boy I was mentoring at the time, to join me and my parents to greet voters as they approached the polling sites. I also took the opportunity to teach Angel about civics and the importance of voting, caring about the community, and doing good, honest work.

That night, I was officially elected to the Board of Education with 4,522 votes. That is a good vote count for a newbie without any political experience or name recognition. I was also the only Hispanic candidate and the youngest to run and be elected in this race. I believe I was also the first Paraguayan-American to be elected to a political position.

I am honored to have served the town of Wallingford, Connecticut, and my hope for the future is that more young people see the value and see the value of giving their time to make tomorrow better.

I can't take full credit for being the youngest and only Hispanic candidate to run in this election. I had a team of exceptional supporters reinforcing and championing me along my first political journey, including my campaign manager Jeff Necio, my mentors Bob Parisi and Steve Knight, and my family and friends who showed support for me at my fundraiser. We hustled and worked hard, and the voters in our community saw potential and put their faith in someone new.

I learned a lot about politics, city budgets, and the red tape and restrictions of government. At the end of my term, I tallied more than 325 hours of unpaid community service I invested into the town of Wallingford and the children's education. The time was divided between expulsion hearings, speaking engagements, the monthly televised and weekly non-televised meetings, and all the other hiring interviews and special session meetings.

What I loved best about my experience was truly feeling like I made a difference in our town's education system. I also saw how blessed the town of Wallingford was to have a bipartisan board that truly put the kids first.

Although I have hung up my political cap, I am committed to being open to new opportunities. I wish to continue to be a conduit helping to lift up our young people so they can reach success and find happiness.

Exercise

1. How have you most effectively given back to your community?

    _____

    _____

    _____

    _____

    _____

2. Describe your experience with mentorship. Would you do it again?

    _____

    _____

    _____

    _____

    _____

Defying the Odds

Some women like to flow with the norms of society while others like to go against the grain and defy the odds. Winsome Sears of Virginia is a well-educated woman who established a business using her training as an electrician to help her community. She is a Republican politician who understands how vital small businesses are to our country.

Sears has achieved several impressive accomplishments that make women all over proud:

1. Female veteran (U.S Marine Corp)
2. Legal immigrant woman from Jamaica
3. First Black woman elected to a statewide political position
4. First Black woman to be elected to Lieutenant Governor of the Old Dominion State

Sears' life isn't solely centered on politics. Some of her greatest accomplishments include her lovely family, her work in the community as the director of a women's shelter for the Salvation Army, and her men's prison ministry. She hopes young people look at her and say, "If Winsome Sears can do it, so can I."

Exercise

1. How can you pay more attention to your local government and the policies that effect you?

_____

_____

_____

_____

2. What does civic duty mean to you?

_____

_____

_____

_____

_____

Breaking Barriers

Breaking barriers is not an easy feat. Not only was Jackie Robinson a talented athlete, but he was a courageous champion for equality on and off the field. Prior to his baseball career, he took a stand for equal rights when he refused to move to the back of a segregated bus while he was serving in the Army. He was arrested, acquitted of all charges, and honorably discharged from the Army.

Robinson began as a shortstop for the Kansas City Monarchs. Then he joined the Montreal Royals in 1946. He was promoted to the Dodgers and made his big-league debut on April 15, 1947. Despite being a Black man in what was then a white sport, he was named the National League MVP and received the inaugural Baseball Writers' Association of America's Rookie of the Year Award.

Every season on April 15, major league baseball teams celebrate Jackie Robinson Day. It commemorates the day Jackie became the first Black player in the American or National League.

Jackie Robinson even inspired and paved the way for Martin Luther King, Jr., who said, "Jackie Robinson made my success possible." His courage inspired many others like Bill Russell, who played professional basketball and stood up against inequities within that sport. Robinson was inducted into the Hall of Fame in 1962 and passed away ten years later. During his time with the Dodgers, they won six pennants and Robinson had a .342 batting average.

Robinson was not only talented but had a great demeanor that served him well when people weren't physically and mentally abusive. From teammates to crowds, he and his family were routinely threatened, but he focused on being great at baseball, and he changed history by breaking a barrier. His legacy, name, and courage will live on as a symbol of triumph and the need for racial equality.

Exercise

1. Describe a prejudice your parents or grandparents had. Have you been able to change your perspective?

    _____

    _____

    _____

    _____

    _____

    _____

2. Have you ever had a meal with a person of color or someone who was culturally different from you? If not, why not?

_____

_____

_____

_____

_____

Working Together

Melissa and Doug Bernstein are a match made in toy heaven. They have been together for thirty years and counting. Since both had educators for parents, they had a knack for creativity and teaching. So, naturally, their segue into creating the largest toy company in the world and creating meaningful products for children to inspire creative thinking and exploration makes total sense.

The mission of Melissa & Doug, LLC, is to provide a launch pad to ignite imagination and a sense of wonder in all children so they can discover themselves, their passions, and their purpose. Doug and Melissa have created roughly 5,000 products, and their innovations and beliefs are a big reason the AAP (American Academy of Pediatrics) joined forces with the Bernsteins to spread awareness of the health benefits of play.

Melissa and Doug Bernstein believe there are five solid reasons to believe in the power of free play:

1. **Play Reveals Passions:** Children need the opportunity to discover their passions and talents. Play allows them the chance to figure out who they are and what they love to do, setting them up to tap into their core selves.

2. **Play Promotes Creativity and Problem Solving:** When children are not overstimulated, they will gravitate to creativity and creative thinking.

3. **Play Develops Resilience and Grit:** Play allows children to have the freedom of trial and error.

4. **Play Builds Social Skills:** Interacting with adults and friends while playing allows children to experience the social terrain, learn norms, develop empathy, negotiate, and develop many other skills.

5. **Play Sharpens Cognitive Skills:** Children learn about the world through play, and it helps them develop their brains, language, and confidence.

The innocence and beauty of a child's mind is something so special that we must preserve it. As adults, we can be mindful of how we interact with children and what type of activities and toys we give them. If we allow their bodies and minds to have the space to roam and be creative, we will set them and our future up for success.

Exercise

1. What is your most memorable play moment from your childhood?

    _____

    _____

    _____

2. If you could design any child product, what would it be?

    _____

    _____

    _____

3. Describe a memory of you playing as a child that brought you joy. Is there
    a way you can incorporate a similar activity and joy as an adult, or can you
    share this activity with your children or nieces and nephews? (For exam-
    ple, visit some place whimsical like ice castles in New Hampshire, attend
    adult camp, go to a retreat, or just schedule an afternoon in your backyard
    looking for bugs, building a fort, and playing hide-and-go-seek).

    _____

    _____

    _____

    _____

    _____

Summary

Challenging the system, societal norms, our fast-paced digital lives, and the way things are is not for the faint of heart. It takes courage, innovation, and a vision to make a change, be the first, and champion a new way of thinking, doing, and being. Each of us can do many things to foster a better way of living. What will you contribute to society?

AMANDA MOTTOLA

CHAPTER 16
KISSING THE BULLY GOODBYE

"I've been actually really very pleased to see how much awareness was raised around bullying and how deeply it affects everyone. You know, you don't have to be the loser kid in high school to be bullied. Bullying and being picked on comes in so many different forms."

— Lady Gaga

You just heard some amazing overcoming the status quo stories. Now let's talk about bullies. The bully is a metaphor for traditional corporate life, and we also face real-life bullies of all shapes and sizes from childhood on. Never subject yourself to negative treatment, being victimized, or enduring toxic environments. Life is short, and bullies will drain the life out of you and damage your health if you let them. Cheers to kissing the bullies goodbye!

Combatting Bullies

Selena Gomez is a talented and beautiful Hispanic singer and actress. However, she is not immune to being bullied. Gomez suffers from lupus and takes her health seriously because her autoimmune disease can be debilitating. She has been ridiculed for weight fluctuations even though lupus causes weight loss and weight gain either from the medication or associated digestive problems. In a *Billboard* interview, Gomez said, "Imagine all the insecurities you already feel about yourself and having someone write a paragraph pointing out every little thing—even if it's just physical."

Below are the three most common types of bullying people experience. All of them can wreak havoc on a person's psyche.

- Physical bullying: The victim experiences physical or attempted physical harm to their body.

- Verbal bullying: The victim experiences verbal threats and teasing.

- Social bullying: The victim experiences their reputation or relationships being destroyed.

Gomez has taken action by spreading awareness about bullying through her role as executive director of the series *Thirteen Reasons Why* on Netflix, which is an adaptation of Jay Asher's book. Gomez is on a mission to be a part of projects that have meaning. She continues to inspire and be a great role model for women all over the world.

It is important to be strong in both your body and your mind so you can combat the bullies you may encounter. I challenge you to take a week off from social media to detox and avoid getting hit with all the ads and pressure to have, be, or feel a certain way. During this time, try some Lumosity brain games, put together a puzzle, or play a game of chess to strengthen your mind and enjoy life away from the screen and knowing what everybody else is doing.

Exercise

1. Why would someone judge someone else online whom they have never met? When was the last time you did this?

    _____

    _____

    _____

    _____

2. Next time you are on social media, set a timer so you can create a healthier relationship with social media and preserve one of your most precious assets—your time. How much time did you spend? Are you surprised?

    _____

    _____

    _____

    _____

Bullying Is Never the Answer

It all started with a tall, skinny boy I had a crush on as a junior in high school. We made out downstairs on the couch in between my mother loudly sneaking downstairs to do another load of "laundry." (Mom, if you are reading this, I know you were checking up on me.) Unfortunately, he had a girlfriend even though he said he didn't. As you can imagine, the other girl wasn't thrilled and started plotting revenge on me.

At the time, the cool thing was Tom Anderson's MySpace, and I, of course, like all my friends, had a page, and so did my bully. She began posting that I was short, fat, and ugly. For a female teen, those are the three most devastating words to hear, especially when plastered online for the world to see. I was crying not only in the Lauralton Hall bathroom stall but when I got home from school. My girlfriends were there for me, but these hurtful posts were depressing. Then the post became threatening, with one saying, "I want to beat her up."

One of my favorite English teachers, Mrs. Boynton heard about it and out of concern told my mom, who printed the posts and wanted to bring them to the police to file a harassment report. However, that would have been embarrassing, and at this time, there wasn't much legislation or protocol yet for online bullying, so I took matters into my own hands and confronted the bully.

I was scared of her, but deep down, I knew it would only get worse if I didn't take a stand. I knew in my heart that this young woman must be a good person deep down, despite her hurtful words. We ended up talking on the phone for a good hour. She explained her frustration with me, and I apologized for her hurt and forgave her for the pain she had caused me. We ended up learning about each other, and I am proud of having stood up for myself and being able to forgive. Often, hurt people hurt other people. I came to understand she wasn't mad at me. I just got caught in the crossfire of her anger at the skinny boy. Most importantly, she apologized, and I wholeheartedly forgave her. We both agreed skinny guy was no good for either of us and that we'd each had a lapse of judgment when it came to him. To this day, we are cool with each other. I hold no ill feelings toward her—she is a great person and mom. My bullying story ended in a powerfully positive way with apologies and forgiveness. However, for many, that is not the case. According to "Stop Cyberbullying Before It Starts," at the National Crime Prevention Council's website, only one in ten teen victims of bullying will inform a parent or adult of the abusive experience. (Accessed July 30, 2019.)

If you or someone you know is being bullied, there are ways you can get help.

- Text "Hello" to 741741 to connect with a crisis counselor.

- Tell a teacher or trusted adult.

- Find new friends who help lift you up not break you down. Get involved in a new activity to meet some new people.

- Check yourself if you are the one picking on someone else. Dig deep to find out why you are doing this.

Exercise

1. Describe a time when you witnessed bullying. How did you react then, and is it different from how you would react now?

   _____

   _____

   _____

2. I challenge you to think about a time you may have intentionally or un-
    intentionally mistreated someone. Write them a letter of apology. Then
    write another letter to someone who may have hurt you and forgive
    them for the hurt they caused—use this opportunity to free yourself
    from the burden on your heart.

    _____

    _____

    _____

    _____

Making Magic From Fire

Are you familiar with the Harry Potter books, the seven-part fantasy book
series that took the world by storm? Harry's wizarding world has captured
the hearts and imaginations of millions of people, and the books have sold
more than 500 million copies.

Joanne Rowling (aka J. K. Rowling) was not always the mother of the Harry
Potter series as we know her today. She did, however, always have a passion
for books and began writing at a young age. Her extensive reading not only
racked up some book fees at the library, but she was able to expand her
knowledge into the realm of Latin, which paved the way for the base of
the spells in her Harry Potter books. While working as an administrator,
she was caught crafting stories on her work computer and was fired. However, this ended up being a blessing in disguise for her, despite the initial

hardship it caused. She was able to make magic from being fired, and her success has inspired people from all over the world.

> "Why do I talk about the benefits of failure? Simply because failure meant a stripping away of the inessential. I stopped pretending to myself that I was anything other than what I was and began to direct all my energy into finishing the only work that mattered to me."
>
> — J.K. Rowling

In 1990, Rowling turned an idea that came to her in transit from Manchester to London into magic with her imagination and words.

Today, her books are admired by people of all ages around the world, and she has become one of the most successful and influential authors. Being a teenager or an adult in the public eye has its benefits, but it can also open your life, words, and thoughts to be scrutinized and judged. Over the years, Rowling has also experienced the effects of bullying. In 2011, Rowling wrote back in response to a particular fan's letter acknowledging the teen's experience and sharing her own feelings on the topic.

"I know what it is like to be picked on, as it happened to me, too, throughout my adolescence," Rowling said. "Being a teenager can be completely horrible." More recently, in 2020, she was bullied and digitally harassed for her opinions in a gender discussion.

As Lady Gaga said in this chapter's opening quote, bullying doesn't just happen to popular or unpopular people; it can happen to anyone at any time. Hearing from people in the limelight who have experienced bullying is important to shedding light on the frequency and devastation that bullying can cause. Let's all work together to be kinder to each other and to take the hurt we have experienced in our lives and convert it into positive energy before passing along the hurt to someone else.

Let's focus on passing on kindness and using our gifts to pass along some magic to others lives.

Exercise

1. If you were laid off or fired tomorrow, what would you do next?

2. Is there a bully you need to kiss goodbye?

Dipping Fruit No More

Have you ever dipped a piece of pineapple or a strawberry in chocolate? At first, they look like something out of Salvador Dali's imagination on par with his melting clocks. However, if you leave that narrow box we sometimes put ourselves in and try something as simple as dipping fruit (or as complex as changing jobs), big things can happen.

I may have been a bit crazy to leave a job where I had paid maternity leave and great labor and delivery benefits when I was three-months pregnant. However, I can confidently say that while you are never ready to have a baby, you always know when you are ready for the next chapter in your career. Don't ignore your gut! As much as I enjoyed pieces of my previous job, it wasn't enough for me to stay. I saw the bigger picture, and my focus going forward would 100 percent be growing my family and following my passion and purpose. Although a new job was a bit of a risk and I really didn't want to be that new, friendless, pregnant chick, I knew in my heart it was a much-needed leap of faith, and I was doing it for my soon-to-be son.

After running a gauntlet of interviews with multiple vice presidents, I graciously accepted a job at Edible Arrangements' corporate headquarters in Wallingford, Connecticut. I worked in project management on the innovation team. Unfortunately, four months into my job, we learned the company was relocating to Atlanta, which was a hub of franchise headquarters with a great pool of applicants. And it's way cheaper to operate a business in the South than in New England. For the company, this transition made absolute sense, but for me, it did not.

My opportunity for an even better future didn't arrive until Luca was born a few months later and an even better story began to unfold.

I always thought the corporate world was my friend. My goals centered around moving up the proverbial ladder. However, as the clock ticked closer to meeting my little man, my confidence in working for someone else waned. I found myself fantasizing about what I would do after I became unemployed. Would I be a stay-at-home mom, climb mountains, be a Poshmark or eBay reselling guru and find a way to feed my hungry entrepreneurial spirit?

I enjoy working, but I thought I might dial it back so I could be there fully for my son. I felt as though the world was my oyster, and I was ready to indulge in a tasty dream—the dream of being my own boss, being a stellar mom, and kissing the bully (the corporate world) goodbye.

Even though I was a bit concerned about not having a secure income, the layoff showed me that my confidence in a bi-weekly paycheck and working for someone else was a facade anyway. As scary as it was to step off the corporate ladder, it felt like a burden had been lifted from my shoulders. I had this sense of happiness and excitement. Even though the paycheck went away, along with the benefits, I was okay with it. That is when the yellow brick road lit up, and it has continued to be paved in front of me one brick at a time.

Deciding to feed my entrepreneurial spirit and take the risk of opening my own marketing agency, Otraway, has been one of my greatest successes and afforded me the opportunity to spend unlimited time with my children.

Exercise

1. Do you love your current job? If so, why? If not, why are you there?

    _____

    _____

    _____

    _____

2. How can you step out of your comfort zone this week both profession-
    ally and personally?

    _____

    _____

    _____

    _____

Summary

The bully in your life may not be obvious, but if you dive in deeply and
see what or who is holding you back, your life will be transformed. Is it
a person, a job, or yourself? The first step in kissing the bully goodbye is
understanding what is plaguing you and coming up with a game plan. You
deserve to do exactly what you were meant to do. So go get it and kiss the
bully goodbye!

CHAPTER 17
CLIMBING YOUR MOUNTAINS

"Every mountain top is within reach if you just keep climbing."

— Barry Finlay

In the last chapter, we talked about kissing the bully goodbye. Now, hold your breath as we dive into some amazing stories about climbing mountains. In our lives, there are figurative and literal mountains that may seem insurmountable at times, but the forthcoming stories will inspire you to take on the biggest mountains because…why the heck not? Regardless of a fear of heights, being unmotivated, out of shape, or overly cautious, let's throw caution to the wind and get to climbing. The summit is waiting!

Testing Love in Nature

Has someone you liked ever pushed you out of your comfort zone? Have you ever climbed mountains for someone you love? Well, I have officially done both and survived to tell the tales.

For our one-year dating anniversary in 2009, Pete planned what I was told would be a romantic Labor Day camping weekend in gorgeous New Hampshire. If you knew me back then, you would know my version of camping included a beach, a bed, and a bathroom, or at the very least, some form of luxury glamping. However, I knew Pete could be my guy, so I vowed to give this nature thing a try. I do dabble in some outdoorsy activities and excursions, but I am by no means meant to go on a survival weekend without any mental or physical preparation.

The preparations for this "romantic, easy, and fun" trip began with several warning signs that I absently dismissed as being normal protocol for a weekend in New Hampshire. The first sign was the bag full of MREs we purchased. For non-survivalists, Meals Ready-to-Eat are dehydrated meals that should only be used in the event of a natural disaster or zombie apocalypse. The second warning was that Pete packed only one headlamp and sleeping bag. The third warning was that he mentioned nonchalantly that we would drop our car off on one side of the mountains and take a shuttle to the other side, hike some mountains, and arrive back at our car. The keyword here being the plural mountains.

Day 1: The shuttle dropped us off on the opposite side of the mountain range from our car. The moment the shuttle bid us adieu, I had a brief freak-out moment, but I decided not to let it show. I did, however, eat all the chocolate-covered pretzel sticks his mom had packed for me before we even hiked a few miles. The first watering station was a short hike. I thought we would sleep in the little hut nearby, but Pete beckoned me to keep hiking.

We got to a small clearing about half a mile past the water station and set up camp. I was useless by this point, so he told me to relax while he pitched the tent. It was already frigid out, and I quickly realized I did not pack properly.

We weren't even at that high of an elevation yet.

Night fell and we ate our first dehydrated meal—a Bolognese pasta. I was famished and pleasantly surprised by it. I thought the hike wasn't going to be so bad. Pete then accidentally knocked over most of our water. If we wanted more, we would have to walk a half mile in the dark. I heard some animals, so I passed on the walk. Fortunately, we had enough water to brush our teeth, and then we hit the sack.

The sack was less than desirable. It was one sleeping bag on top of jagged rocks. We had no padding beneath us. Pete suggested that we both put our feet and legs in the sleeping bag, so I sat down on his lap and wiggled into the sleeping bag. He said he would bear-hug me to keep me warm since the sleeping bag was only keeping our lower half warm. I sarcastically muttered, "How romantic." We used our packs as pillows. It was definitely one of the worst sleeping arrangements of my life.

Day 2 a.m.: We started the day off with Pete running up to the spigot to get some water for coffee and our breakfast. I was starving so I was excited for the one dehydrated meal I picked—huevos rancheros. I was anticipating a tasty breakfast. He came back with the water, and I added it to my breakfast. I took a heaping spoonful of the dehydrated monstrosity, and to my dismay, it was horrible.

While we ate, Pete ran through our itinerary for the day. It consisted of hiking to Mount Washington and having lunch at the weather station at the top. He said it like it was no big deal. I didn't know until after the trip that Mount Washington was the highest elevation in New England. After hiking seven miles and then up Mount Washington, I was pretty spent and starving. My virgin hiking legs ached and my back hurt from carrying the forty-pound pack.

Day 2 p.m.: The view from the top of Mount Washington was a bit cloudy, and it was cold. We went into the Adams Visitor Center to warm up. I was famished, so my prepacked tuna sandwich tasted like a gift from God.

While inside, we saw a weather report warning of severe weather. You see, multiple weather spheres meet at the top of Mount Washington, so it can change from sunny to treacherous in minutes. The weather report at the conservatory called for flash flooding and torrential downpours, which can be deadly for hikers. Not to mention, our car was parked adjacent to a riverbed.

I looked at Pete. He looked more serious than usual and said, "Well, that changes our plans. It is a little after 1 p.m., so we have three choices. We can stay in the tent, which would be uncomfortable and wet. The little huts are all booked, so we can try to sleep on the floor at one, or we can night hike, which can be dangerous, but the flash flooding tomorrow can also pose some risks. It may take up to ten hours for us to make it back to the car, but we can do it."

All I could think was, *What did I get myself into?* After weighing our options, we decided to go back to the car. We quickly finished our meal, filled our canteens, and prepared for the hike.

We began the descent down Mount Washington around 2:45 p.m. It wasn't bad at first, but then my knees began to ache. We kept pushing forward, one step after another. I was beginning to feel like Sisyphus with all this effort and seemingly no progress. Pete could tell I was losing steam and immediately reminded me that we were almost there—even though we still had hours to go. Unlike Sisyphus' story, there was a light at the end of the Crawford Notch Path for us, and I visualized us safe and sound in his Pontiac.

The thing I liked about hiking was all the friendly faces and the dogs. We saw a lot of people until about 6:30 p.m. After that, we didn't see anyone else hiking. It was kind of eerie being alone at the mercy of nature without any shelter—something I have never experienced before.

It felt like an endless trek. Would we ever make it to the car? I tripped and twisted my ankle. I was already slowing down and exhausted, so Pete took my pack and carried both.

We needed to step up the pace to minimize the night hiking. We hiked one last mountain before getting to Crawford Path. As we entered the ever-green-lined trail about 8 p.m., the sun was setting and then night arrived—it was pitch black. With only one head lamp, we had to take turns leading the way. I found out later that if you are not properly packed with safety gear (e.g., one headlight per person hiking) and need to be rescued, you get whacked with a negligence bill.

We continued for about three or four more hours. It felt like we were trapped in the Twilight Zone; the trail looked the same everywhere, and I had zero point of reference. At one point, we thought we were lost. Not only was it pitch black with only one faint beam of light from our head lamp, but the rocks on the trail were wet and slippery—and we heard animals all around us. Pete saw a bear paw print on one of the rocks. I was scared.

When I slipped again, the waterworks went off, and I felt defeated. I told Pete to go on without me. I was so tired, but he got me up and we continued.

We finally saw some faint lights through the trees and realized it was the Mount Washington Hotel. We were so relieved; the hotel meant we were only about a mile from the road and our car. We kept walking and made it to the road shortly after 11 p.m. I collapsed on the road in tears. I hugged the pavement like it was an old friend and sobbed.

We went to the car, both of us looking pretty beat up. I was shivering and pretty sure I had developed a fever. Pete couldn't move his arms because he had been carrying the two packs and his back and arm muscles had locked from the tension and weight, and we just sat in the car in silence.

Then Pete asked if I wanted to sleep in the car. I screamed, "Hell no! Get me to a hotel, now; you owe me that. This was so far from romantic."

I felt like Mary and Joseph because every hotel was closed. We finally rolled up to the Shakespeare Inn, which was open. We went in and told the innkeeper about our journey. He gave us two free sodas and led us to our room. The soda was delicious, and we both collapsed in one of the double beds despite being filthy. It felt like heaven.

After a brief rest, we showered and went to bed happy to be alive and warm.

We had hiked a total of twenty miles—hiking Mounts Adams, Jefferson,

Washington, and Monroe. Looking back at this not-so-romantic adventure, I know I should have asked more questions about the itinerary, picked up on the red flags, and packed a second sleeping bag and headlamp. The trip was a nightmare, but the trek makes for a hysterical and memorable story.

The trip also proved, even with no mountain hiking experience, I could do it and so much more.

I didn't know at the time, but Pete had planned for us to hike the Presidential Traverse, which is about a twenty-three mile portion of New Hampshire's White Mountain Range that includes: Mounts Madison, Adams, Jefferson, Washington, Monroe, Eisenhower, and Pierce. This is a total of seven summits, and includes the highest elevation in New England. I am a bit flattered that Pete thought I was capable of such a feat. Either that or he was testing my stamina or simply trying to kill me. It is a trek that experienced hikers take, not a novice who had only hiked the 739-foot Sleeping Giant in Hamden, Connecticut.

If I hadn't been willing to step far outside my comfort zone, I wouldn't have this fond memory, seen some epic summits, and survived a weekend in nature with few resources. This story even found its way into my maid of honor Eva's speech at our wedding, and we are training to do the Presidential Traverse in 2022. This time we will pack another headlamp just in case, but our plan is to start in the morning and finish the same day. Please send positive vibes, and I will make sure to share how it goes on amandamottola. com and in my next book!

Climbing mountains, overcoming challenges, and surviving to tell the story is what life is all about. Never give up once you begin the climb; you are so much stronger than you realize!

Exercise

1. What was your worst and best experience in nature?

    _____

    _____

    _____

    _____

2. Who inspires you to climb mountains?

    _____

    _____

    _____

    _____

Running to Provincetown

Is there a physical activity you can't stand doing—maybe one that involves sneakers, is monotonous, and is hard on your knees? For me, the only acceptable times to run are when you are being assaulted, trying to score a point in a game, or being chased by a zombie.

I have never been one to run for pleasure. It was always more of a punishment (like extra laps after practice). On a normal day, you wouldn't catch me being part of a relay team doing a 192-mile run. However, I love my family, and my brother Brian needed spots filled on his Cape Cod 2013 Ragnar team. The Ragnar consists of a team of twelve running 192-miles over two days. Pete and I agreed to participate and help my brother out. Pete was more prepared for the endeavor. Me, not so much. I had done some walking and the elliptical at the gym, but I had not trained for this stamina-focused race.

During the race, a quote from Dag Hammarskjold ran through my head: "Never look down to test the ground before taking your next step; only he who keeps his eye fixed on the far horizon will find the right road." I wanted to give up several times, but I kept my eye on the horizon—or in this case, the beer and chowder at the end of the race.

We began our run at 8:30 a.m. on Friday and finished on Saturday around 5:30 p.m. I was runner number eight, so I had my first run as part of the relay team around three on Friday afternoon. Then I ran at two in the morning on Saturday and again Saturday afternoon around two for a total of fifteen miles.

Between runs, we were crammed into a small van going from checkpoint to checkpoint, and I felt my muscles tightening up. My night run was cool and peaceful. At some points, it was a little scary running in the total darkness with my blinking butt light, reflective vest, and headlamp, but I enjoyed it overall, even though it was only thirty-nine degrees out. The lack of sleep and uncomfortable living conditions of the race sucked, but I was able to suck it up and finish.

It was great to be part of a twelve-person team, and all the participants in the relay race were so supportive. At times, I felt like I couldn't run another step, but someone would pass me and say, "You're almost there; you got this," and that was the little boost I needed. It was great to see so much support, even though it was technically a competition. My team finished by Saturday evening and averaged ten-minute miles. I honestly didn't think I would finish the fifteen-plus miles in those conditions, but I did, and I impressed myself. I used to be the chunky little asthmatic girl who couldn't run for anything, but I completed this feat with my best running times ever, and I felt great! Although they ran out of chowder by the time we finished the race, the thought of having it really kept me going. To combat my disappointment, Pete took me to get chowder after the race, and it was the best tasting prize I have ever had.

Our bodies are capable of so much while we are young, but one day, we will get older and face physical limitations, so I plan to keep working on improving my fitness and agility because if you don't care for your body, who else will?

Exercise

1. What is the hardest workout you have ever done? How did you feel afterward?

_____

_____

_____

_____

2. What can you do this week to level up your fitness routine?

_____

_____

_____

_____

Breaking the Cycle

Do you know what the top ten poorest countries in the world have in common? They are all in Africa. The poverty in these countries is intense, and people lack the very things essential for survival: water, food, and shelter.

Pat Stevenson Doerr (aka my mom) had the privilege of visiting Malawi back in 2012, and it was a life-changing experience. One friendship that changed her life was meeting eighteen-year-old Emily Chimbalanga. Emily's parents both passed away in 2005, leaving her and her four siblings orphaned. Her grandmother took them in and supported Emily and her four siblings (two brothers and two sisters) and helped them attend school.

Pat learned a lot about Emily. Emily's typical day began at 4 a.m. when she went to the well with a twenty-liter jug to get water; she carried it back on her head. She then prepared a porridge made from maize and salt for herself and her siblings. After breakfast, it was time for school. Emily walked fifteen miles to school, which started at 7:30 a.m. She was a sophomore in high school and studied biology, English, life skills, Bible knowledge, physical science, geography, math, and Chichewa (a Bantu language spoken in much of southern, southeast, and east Africa). Unlike teachers in the United States who need a degree in teaching and must consistently stay up to date through professional development and continuing education, Emily's teachers were just willing amateurs. Her class consisted of about 150 students divided between two rooms.

Emily attended school until 3 p.m. and then walked another fifteen miles back home. She usually got home by 6 p.m. and prepared nsima with footso (porridge made from corn with dried pumpkin leaves for relish) for dinner. Then she'd study and go to bed. She also encouraged her siblings to complete their assignments.

The village Orphan and Vulnerable Children Committee provided legal assistance and a little food. They managed and supported fifty children in the village. Despite this life of serving and caring for her family, Emily has always been committed to her education and being successful. No matter where you live, hard work and dedication to a dream are prevalent among people. It is important to remember that all over the world others are climbing mountains every day so they can one day get to the summit—a better life.

Exercise

1. What was the longest walk of your life? How far could you walk every day if you had to?

    _____

    _____

    _____

    _____

2. How have you cared for a loved one?

    _____

    _____

    _____

    _____

Mountaineering Fourteen Peaks

Although my mountain-climbing experience was pretty harrowing for me, it seems like a cake walk compared to the experience of Nirmal Purja, the Nepali mountaineer featured in the Netflix documentary *14 Peaks: Nothing Is Impossible*. This next-level crazy adventure was about summiting fourteen of the world's 8,000-meter peaks in seven months.

Eight-thousand meters is about 26,246 feet (almost five miles). The documentary sheds light on the beauty and danger of the mountains and Nirmal

Purja's commitment to his 2019 mission, Project Possible. A twenty-kilometer journey with a seventy-five-pound pack is a normal daily run for this larger-than-life person, who shows his kind and giving nature by pausing to help others along the way.

It takes determination and commitment to embark on something others deem impossible. Here is a run-down of what Purja accomplished.

Phase 1: Nepal—Purja set a world record by climbing Everest, Lhotse, and Makalu in forty-eight hours.

Phase 2: Pakistan—Summit K2 is in the Himalayan mountain range, which is the second-highest mountain in the world. It is even more dangerous to climb than Mount Everest despite Everest being taller.

Phase 3: Climb in Tibet—For Purja to successfully complete his Project Possible, he had to climb Shishpangma in Tibet. However, this climb requires a permit from China, which he was initially denied. Courageous and determined, Purja petitioned Chinese officials and took to social media, inspiring his followers to write to the Chinese government to demand they give him access to the mountain. He was successful, and on October 29, 2019, he reached the summit of Shishpangma.

In summiting the fourteen peaks in six months and six days, Purja accomplished the single greatest mountaineering feat in history.

Exercise

1. Would you ever climb Mount Everest? Why or why not?

_____

_____

_____

_____

2. What is the most strenuous mental and physical mountain you ever climbed?

_____

_____

_____

_____

Summary

Climbing a mountain can be a long and tedious undertaking. Sometimes it is hard not to straddle the dark side and be super-pessimistic. Life can be cruel and funny in the sense that it can kick you when you're down. It can be hard to fight back, but you must let your inner strength come into play because while there will always be an abundance of detours that might be easier, you risk missing out on learning exactly what you are made of and experiencing the stunning view from the top if you don't follow through. The climb isn't meant to be easy because then we might take the vast beauty and tranquility of the summits for granted. Anything worth having is worth the climb.

CHAPTER 18

CREATING YOUR OWN DESTINY

"It is not in the stars to hold our destiny but in ourselves."

— Shakespeare

We looked at some serious mountain climbing in the last chapter. Now let's bear witness to some amazing stories of people creating their own destinies to gain some inspiration for how we can create our very own destiny.

Seizing the Opportunity

It was a Friday afternoon at the University of New Haven. I had one more class before the weekend kicked off. While running an errand, I popped into Dunkin' Donuts before heading to my legal writing class. I bumped into my classmate Chris Henderson. He asked if I had submitted my application for the President's Public Service Fellowship. I said, "No. What the heck is that?" He said it was offered by the university to place students in a fellowship program (internship) for the upcoming summer. The students selected would work at a non-profit in the New Haven area that matched their major and future career path. It would be a phenomenal opportunity that included a stipend and room and board, but only for ten or so individuals. I was immediately hooked on the idea of being in the program. If it were exclusive or prestigious, I wanted in, or at the very least, I would fail trying. Chris could tell I was interested and told me the application was due that day by 3:00 p.m.

My heart sank because it sounded like an insurmountable feat to fill out the application thoroughly and get two to three references. However, if I have my heart set on being one of ten, I will be one of the ten.

I glanced at my phone and saw I only had four hours. Chris, being the prepared future attorney I knew he was, pulled out a pristine copy of the application for me. It was serendipitous, almost like he knew I hadn't applied.

I immediately mapped out the timeline in my head, working back from 3:00 p.m. I would obviously need to start and possibly finish the application during my research and legal writing class, which was about to start. I would also need to email my references when I first sat down so they had a few hours to get me what I needed. Fortunately, my law class was in the computer lab right next to Dunkin' Donuts, so I saved time by not having to trek across campus.

Unfortunately, giving my busy professors a mere four hours to craft a referral for this program on a Friday afternoon was a bit inconsiderate. I shook off the negative thoughts, knowing the individuals I was asking truly believed in my ability to do great things, respected me, and wanted to see me succeed, so they would be happy to help me in a pinch.

I emailed Donna Morris, my paralegal certificate advisor and one of my law professors. I was president of the legal society and a good student in Donna

Morris' class, so I knew she would be willing to help. I crafted a quick request for a referral and hit send. Next, I was 97 percent sure I would ask my accounting professor Mary Miller for a reference. Even though I was only a C student in her class, I participated and tried, so I knew she liked me.

The last person I asked for a reference was Dennis Blader, my communications professor. Yes, the one I mentioned previously—we still are friends. After class, at about 1:30 p.m., I went around to the various buildings collecting my references and finalizing my application. All three of the professors came through, and my application was complete. With a sweaty palm and brow, I proudly handed my application to Mr. Martin O'Connor in the criminal justice building.

I forgot about the fellowship, and honestly, I think some of my confidence may have waned since I had no clue how many had applied, nor if my application looked like I had put it together at the last minute, so after a little while, my defense was to back-burner the prospect. Then I got an email saying I had been selected. Chris and I both got a spot, and we were eager to begin.

The University of New Haven placed a lot of value in experiential education, and this Fellowship was an exceptional program. I was placed at the Greater New Haven Chamber of Commerce, and it was one of the best experiences of my career at UNH. While there, I:

- Joined PULSE, a young professional organization, and later went on to be on its board of directors.

- Met Amy Neale (also a University of New Haven Alumnus) who later inspired me to start consulting and sent me my first Otraway client. She is on track to become the Otraway COO.

- Met Steve Gentile and TJ Andrews, who were my first marketing agency bosses, and through their company, I met Gia Vacca, who became my mentor and inspired me to go big with Otraway.

- Gained confidence, which led to Tony Rescigno and Sue Rapini taking me under their wings and teaching me the importance of hard work, networking, and business.

I am a big believer in destiny and seizing opportunity. This experience created some key connections that changed the trajectory of my life and career. I am forever grateful.

Exercise

1. When was the last time you were up against a crazy deadline? How did you handle it?

    _____

    _____

    _____

    _____

2. How can you better handle pressure next time you are faced with a stressful situation?

_____

_____

_____

_____

Rehabbing Your Life

Trent Shelton, former NFL football player turned motivational speaker, is proof that if you keep climbing, you can have success and more. Some of his best-known quotes are: "Don't die with your dreams," and "It all starts with you!"

Shelton had dreams of an NFL career, and he made it. However, it was short-lived because destiny had other plans. Shelton was a free agent in 2007. He played for several teams, but he was plagued by recurring injuries. Being a man of faith, it is no surprise he found his passion for motivating others at church, and it was enough to change his journey. He went on to touch the lives of millions through his words.

Shelton began creating inspirational YouTube videos to help others realize their worth and inner strength. These videos always ended with his signature phrase, "It's rehab time," and spawned a massive community of followers.

"Rehab time is about rehabbing your life. It's about becoming the person you are capable of being, the person you were destined to become," Shelton said.

Shelton is an amazing father to his son Tristan, and he lives life fully in honor of his best friend who committed suicide. These monumental moments lit a fire under Shelton to truly live life and be a better man. His motivation pushed him to seek out his purpose and touch the lives of millions with his words and energy. He also just launched the Rare Breed Academy, which is a six-week program crafted to improve mental, physical, and spiritual wellness.

Exercise

1. Is it currently rehab time for you? What part of your life needs some TLC?

   _____

   _____

   _____

   _____

   _____

2. What small self-care step can you take today?

   _____

   _____

   _____

   _____

   _____

Creating Social Change

Have you ever heard of a social enterprise? This concept is becoming very popular and making a big difference in the economy as entrepreneurs and consumers of all ages become more conscious of where products come from, how they are sold, and how a given company affects their community and beyond.

One of my favorite quotes related to social change is from Martin Luther King, Jr.. He said, "Everybody can be great...because anybody can serve. You don't have to have a college degree to serve. You don't have to make your subject and verb agree to serve. You only need a heart full of grace. A soul generated by love."

Last year, I was accepted into a business accelerator program through the Social Enterprise Greenhouse in Rhode Island. This organization is led by CEO Kelly Ramirez and was developed to create and nurture inclusive entrepreneurial ecosystems that foster just, equitable, and resilient communities. I enjoyed learning about current social enterprises around the country and organizations starting up with the intention of doing good and bettering the lives of others. Everyone in my group had different missions and goals, and it was refreshing to see so many individuals with the drive and desire not only to start something new, but to change the world all in one virtual classroom. It was quite invigorating to be a part of a bigger picture.

My company Otraway is considered a social enterprise because I do my best to use good quality and respectfully made products. I also give back a portion of my profits, help local nonprofits, and do whatever I can to help advance and inspire my community. I also encourage my clients to include a give-back portion in their marketing plans because, without our community and clients, we wouldn't exist. Paying it forward or giving more than we take can reap some seriously great rewards for all.

Here are three great examples of social enterprises in the United States:

The **Chicago Eco House** is an organization created in 2014 by Quilen Blackwell. It employs urban farming, 3D printing, and animal husbandry to provide sustainable opportunities to alleviate poverty. Blackwell had a great upbringing, and when he completed his time in the Peace Corps, he decided to dive into community service. He began tutoring at a high school and witnessed the challenges of extreme inner-city poverty and the detrimental effects it has on the community and young people.

Currently, Chicago has a high rate of unemployment among Black youths sixteen to twenty-four, with about one in four living in poverty. This led Blackwell to create the Chicago Eco House which has four farms in Chicago, one in Detroit, and an in-house flower shop called Southside Blooms. The Chicago Eco house specializes in urban agriculture, which encourages bottom-up economic development. The sacrifices and drive of his family allowed Blackwell to create something special and appreciate life as a social entrepreneur on Chicago's South Side.

Foster Forward was founded about twenty-five years ago in Rhode Island. This organization began as the Rhode Island Foster Parents Association and rebranded in 2012 to offer additional support for young adolescents and adults who are currently or formerly in foster care. It also maintains a storefront that provides gently used clothing, toys, and supplies for foster families. The items are provided at no charge as a resource for all foster families. It has several programs, including the game-changing housing program called Your Way Home program.

Unfortunately, not all foster children find an adoptive family or reunite with their biological family. There comes a point when the state no longer takes responsibility for the young people, and they must leave the foster care system if they are too old. More than 20,000 youth (18-21) each year age out of foster care. Twenty-five percent of these young people experience homelessness within a year of leaving foster care, and half will be homeless within the first four years out of foster care. Foster Forward is striving to disrupt this statistic by rapidly rehousing homeless youth who have aged out of the system through the Your Way Home program.

Everyday Foster Forward is impacting lives. The leadership and staff are committed to supporting children and youth, families, and the child welfare system with the purpose of growing, connecting, improving, and pushing forward.

Toms Shoes is an organization created in 2006 by Blake Mycoskie after a trip to Argentina. He invested $300,000 of his own money into the company and pledged to donate one pair of shoes for every pair he sold. Through this social enterprise, Mycoskie sheds light on global health issues and poverty. According to the "Toms Global Impact Report," Toms Shoes has provided 95 million pairs of shoes to people in eighty-five countries. It also provides clean water and eyeglasses.

Social enterprises are an interesting approach to business and have the power to truly change lives and communities in a profound way. These for-profit and non-profit companies pair business and social solutions to improve the world by solving problems.

Exercise

1. If you were given $100,000 to start a social enterprise, what would it be?

_____

_____

_____

_____

2. Are there social enterprises in your community that you can support?

_____

_____

_____

_____

Empowering the Bichota

I'm going to begin this section by defining the word empower.

1: to give official authority or legal power to. Example: She *empowered* her attorney to act on her behalf.

2: to promote the self-actualization or influence of.

It is also important to define bichota. Singer Karol G's definition of bichota is when you feel sexy, daring, strong, empowered, and like a boss. I think there is a little bit of boss and strength in all of us.

Things don't always unfold the way we want them to, and sometimes we hear things we really don't want to hear. However, sometimes our failed attempts and some constructive criticism are exactly what we need for a reality check. We need to keep tabs on our humbleness, toughen up our skin, and fill our mental resources tool bag for the future.

In college, I really wanted a residential life position on campus, and honestly, my ego thought it was mine for the taking. Boy, was I wrong! At New Haven, students had two job opportunities: residential assistant, better known as an RA (punisher), or academic peer mentor (friend and teacher). Both positions had perks—a meal plan, free room and board, and respect on a resume. I made it through the application process and in-person interview, and just needed to complete the fishbowl-style interview. The fishbowl was a group process where the current staff observed all applicants interacting with each other in small groups to determine which two would best fit in with the current staff. Each group had a collective goal, and the group members had to work as a team to get it done. I was very happy with my participation in the fishbowl activities and knew I was a shoo-in for one of the slots.

Then, I got the email with my rejection. I didn't understand what had happened. I got pretty down on myself when I found out I didn't get either of the positions. Not to toot my own horn, but I did a great job in the fishbowl interview. I took charge when no one else would, delegated, helped the others, participated, and communicated well. I couldn't understand what had happened and thought maybe I had been sent the email by mistake, so I scheduled a follow-up with Becca Kitchell, the head of residential life.

I went to our appointment and asked for feedback on my interview. She pulled out my application, said I did a very good job, and suggested I reapply to be an academic peer mentor my senior year. I was devastated.

I asked her why, if my application and interview were great, I did not get picked? She said sometimes being assertive, a strong communicator, and a leader can intimidate others and rub them the wrong way. She said not everyone reacts well to a strong personality. Although her response hurt my feelings and made me a little angry, I understood she was paying me a compliment and telling me I had done nothing wrong. However, the compliment was an unintentional backhand to my ego.

This humbling experience taught me I can make a great effort, do a good job, and still not achieve my goal—and that is okay. The fill-in, half-year position may have been a terrible experience without team synergy. It may have been terrible for me and the entire team. It only takes one ingredient to change a batch of cookies.

It also reminded me that I am entitled to nothing and need to cut myself some slack because life isn't solely about getting what I want or adding things to my resume. I ended up reapplying my senior year, and it was a wonderful experience.

It's good to be bold. It's good to be strong. It's good to advocate for yourself, ask questions, and seek clarity. Be unapologetically you because there is and never will be anyone else like you for a reason, so leave your mark on the world. Don't sweat it if your resume isn't perfect. Life will pass you by if you are blinded by perfection. Keep plugging away, no matter what.

Exercise

1. Describe a time when you were overlooked for a job. How did you re-cover from it?

    _____

    _____

    _____

    _____

    _____

2. What are the characteristics of an ideal employee? What about an ideal employer?

    _____

    _____

    _____

    _____

    _____

Summary

At times, you will be challenged and think your goal is unattainable. Self-doubt may show up in the form of finances, time, or outlandish fears of the unknown—these are just excuses meant to derail you from following the path to your destiny. However, believe you can create your own destiny by seizing opportunities, rehabbing your life, being a good person, and channeling your inner "bichota." If you don't show up for your life, it most definitely will stop showing up for you. I promise that once you begin accomplishing what you want and overcoming your inner naysayers, the path to your destiny will be illuminated.

Remember, you can do anything.

CHAPTER 19
HEALING YOUR MIND, BODY, AND SOUL

"Early to bed and early to rise makes a man healthy, wealthy and wise."

— Benjamin Franklin

In the last chapter, we talked about creating your destiny. Now we will tackle the three structural pillars of life: your mind, body, and soul. These three pillars are vital to your wellbeing. If they are unstable, you will crumble under life's stress, thereby undermining your health. Health is wealth, and without it, nothing else matters.

Showing Up

Showing up is important, whether it is work, responding to an invitation, a promise, or a decision that requires a commitment. It takes courage to have faith in the universe and let Jesus take the wheel. I love Ron Nehring's quote, "The world is run by those who show up." I wholeheartedly believe your story and success are fueled by staying true to who you are and being present and open to the infinite opportunities in the world that you can take advantage of by just showing up.

My uncle Jon started an awesome talent management company in New York and Los Angeles called Authentic. Consequently, he was always being invited to movie premieres and other celebrity functions. One day, he had two tickets for *The Sisterhood of the Traveling Pants 2* premiere at Manhattan's Ziegfeld Theatre. He had a conflicting appointment and knew I was a fan of the movie—and America Ferrera, his client—so he offered my mom and me his tickets. We obviously said yes, and marked the event with a big star and underlines on our calendar. I was so excited for this event, but I still had to get through a full week of work, which was hard because I was so excited.

On Sunday afternoon, July 20, 2008, I was waiting tables, serving a party of three—a woman, a man, and their son, who must have been in his early twenties. The son was cute, and the family was very sweet. This is my ideal table as a server, the kind that makes slinging drinks and meals more enjoyable. When I dropped off the check, the son handed me a piece of paper. It said, "You are really beautiful. Call me," with his phone number. If he was with a big group of guys, I may have thought he was trying to impress his friends and look like a hot shot. However, since he was with his parents, I thought it was kind of bold and flattering. I admired his courage in asking me out, so I gave him a chance and said yes.

We went out to dinner and things went great, but the next day I had severe food poisoning. Up until then, I had never had food poisoning—it was horrible. I ended up severely dehydrated and my intestines were literally being shredded by e-coli. After hours of excruciating cramps, I ended up in the emergency room. The nurses took fabulous care of me and gave me fluids and some medications to help stop my stomach cramps and nausea. Fortunately,

I was better within a day, but my digestive system had taken a beating. I was so nervous I'd miss the movie premiere. It would be devastating if I missed it. I had until Monday, July 28 to recover. My new beau continued to check in on me, and we went out a few more times, but we eventually lost touch. Even though it wasn't a forever thing for us, I enjoyed his cameo in my life.

After much anticipation, the movie premiere day came, and I was determined to show up. I had a blast with my mom. I got to meet and get a photo with Alexis Bledel, American Ferrera, and Jesse Williams. I saw Chace Crawford, Ed Westwick, Leighton Meester, and Blake Lively, who sat in front of me at the premiere. Unfortunately, at the time, I wasn't familiar with them, so I was not as star-struck as I would have been a few years later when I binged the *Gossip Girl* series.

The after-party was at a rooftop bar in New York with delicious food and champagne, but I wasn't cleared to eat much since my stomach was still recovering. Still, the experience was one I will never forget.

Being healthy one day and terribly ill

the next is scary and really made me think about how quickly our health can change. We don't always have control over who touches our food, but being selective in what we fuel our body with is vital. Also, it is important to have a balance between showing up when we can and allowing our bodies to rest and heal. Our bodies are temples, so maintain them with care.

Exercise

1. Describe a time when you missed a big event because you were sick. Did it make you appreciate your health?

   _____

   _____

   _____

   _____

2. Take a deep breath, clear your mind, and jot down how you feel in this moment. Are you feeling sick, well, sad, happy? How do you aspire to feel?

   _____

   _____

   _____

   _____

Spending Time With Those You Love

Do you spend enough time really being with and engaging with your significant other or the most important people in your life? It is easy to neglect this area or be overly critical of the people closest to us. It is so important to be mindful of how we treat those closest to us and strive to nourish our relationships.

Hugh Jackman is a great actor, human, and companion. He values not only his body, mind, and soul, but his relationships. He has been married to his wife Deborra-Lee Furness for more than twenty-five years. To ensure their relationship stays strong despite their busy schedules, they changed their morning routine to include spending time together to kick off the day. They capitalize on a solid morning routine, reading a book together aloud while sipping tea. This morning ritual is nonnegotiable for them and has become their favorite time of the day. And it sets the day off right, on their terms.

This lovely couple adopted two children after struggling with fertility issues. It was important to them to adopt a biracial child since that is where the biggest need is. Their son Oscar is Cherokee, Hawaiian, African American, and Caucasian, and their daughter Ava is Mexican and German. Spending time with their children and each other is sacrosanct to them. One of Jackman's mantras is, "Happy wife, happy life." I really think he is on to something.

Below are a few ways you can spend enriching time with your family.

- Escape to a museum.
- Start a family book club—whether it is just you and your spouse or the whole family.

- Go for a hike.
- Find a local festival or event to attend.
- Schedule family puzzle and game nights.
- Create a family holiday tradition.

Exercise

1. Does your daily routine include making time for someone special? How can you optimize this time?

2. How can you reinvent your routine to include habits that bring you joy and success?

Healing Postpartum

Having a baby was the most rewarding pain of my life. But it wasn't without trials.

I hit rock bottom somewhere between 2018 and 2019, after having my first baby Luca in the cold New England winter. Pete was working Monday through Friday in a different state, and I had just been laid off. I was recovering from an unplanned C-section that really took the wind out of my sails.

During this time, I was able to build an amazing relationship with my son Luca, stay in a home I wasn't ready to leave, live in a town I loved, successfully breastfeed my baby boy, and start my company called Otraway. However, all this came at the expense of my sanity, my body and mind, and nearly my marriage.

A month into motherhood, I was a mess. My stomach hurt from the Cesarean section whenever I laughed, cried, or sat up—pretty much any movement was misery. Caring for myself was challenging, and caring for Luca was freaking hard even when Pete was home on the weekends.

Life with a baby is a total rollercoaster between the hormones, the new mom bod, and the lack of time for yourself. Not to mention the rift it can create in your marriage because you have no time for each other and you are suffering from a form of torture called sleep deprivation. At times, I felt (sometimes still feel) like a sleep-deprived gremlin. I can't help but grimace when I catch a peek at my weight or the exhaustion staring me down in the mirror.

When Luca was a newborn, I hardly recognized myself. I was frustrated with my weak and recovering body, knowing it would never be the same. I eagerly awaited clearance from my doctor to drive, exercise, bend, and lift something other than Luca. I'm not going to lie and tell you caring for a newborn is easy and will come as naturally as blinking because it doesn't. It's exhausting and will be an omnipresent test of your patience, identity, and marriage.

With that said, I have created a list of the best gifts for mom, dad, and baby postpartum.

- A grocery delivery gift card
- A meal prep service
- A hot or frozen homemade meal
- An Uber Eats or Grubhub gift card
- A postpartum overnight care gift card

On rare occasions, I felt like I was walking on sunshine and handling everything like a super-mom, only to have the rug pulled out from under me. It turned out I had a hidden autoimmune disease festering in my body. My thyroid was attacking itself, causing symptoms I chalked up to parental exhaustion, mom brain, or one of the many other postpartum euphemisms that normalize feelings and symptoms that may be normal but aren't okay.

About seven months postpartum, I started having severe panic attacks. I couldn't breathe, and I felt like I was having a heart attack. I would become confused and stumble over my words. I sometimes questioned if I was having a stroke—or losing my damn mind. This was a challenging and frustrating time, and I felt hopeless, like I was losing pieces of myself.

Fortunately, I had a physical scheduled during this time and my doctor and I figured out I had a thyroid issue. I was temporarily relieved because I had an answer to what was going on, but that morphed into overwhelming feelings of sadness. It was hard to accept that, at thirty, I had a chronic illness that is considered a lifelong condition.

I had to adamantly request to be tested for Hashimoto's because the doctor didn't think it was necessary. It is important to advocate for yourself or postpartum loved ones. You know your body better than anyone else. I ended up having Hashimoto's disease and began my journey to healing and understanding the small butterfly gland in my throat.

Here is a list of the foods I had to remove from my diet to alleviate a Hashimoto's attack.

- Gluten
- Soy
- Dairy
- Products suspected to be endocrine disruptors

I hit a less devastating rock in 2021 after having my second son, Enzo. Cue all the similar feelings and Hashimoto's issues, minus the severe panic attacks and Pete living in a different state during the week. This time was more manageable, and I was more prepared. Some of the things I recommend for any pregnant woman are:

- Doing Pelvic Floor Therapy, which helps with an easier labor and recovery.
- Getting prenatal and postnatal massages for circulation and relaxation.

- Finding a trusted therapist early to combat any postpartum depression and aid in the many changes that come along with an expanding family and changing life.

- Finding a chiropractor for pregnant woman, which helps with overall health and with labor and recovery.

- Walking every day (or doing some exercise okayed by your doctor) is great for mama and baby.

- Getting a good prenatal vitamin. I continue taking mine while breast-feeding as well.

- Hiring a trusted and experienced doula to have additional support during pregnancy, labor, and postpartum.

Despite the whiplash from the good and bad emotions and developing Hashimoto's, I wouldn't change any of the anxiety, fear, frustration, love, happiness, and appreciation for the many struggles of motherhood because without them, I would not have taken control of my health.

Exercise

1. How much water do you drink and which foods do you eat too much of? Could you implement a routine to help you stay better hydrated or fed?

_____

_____

_____

2. What are some ways you can incorporate healthy habits into your cra-
    zy busy parent life? If you aren't a parent, what are some ways you can
    add positive habits to your routine to prepare you for parenthood?

_____

_____

_____

_____

_____

Following a Calling

Life can wreak havoc on people's bodies, minds, and souls. We can all face
dark periods that test us. However, through darkness comes light, and
sometimes the worst times in history give birth to innovation and opportunities.

My client Jeanette Mollis took lemons and made lemonade in 2020, despite
the craziness going on in the world. Before we get into her story, let's step
back a year. In 2019, her son Mikey was born without an immune system.
He underwent bone marrow surgery at Boston Children's Hospital, and
Jeanette and her family had to live in isolation for some time to protect
Mikey from germs while he took forty-plus medications a day in addition
to undergoing seven days of chemotherapy.

While in isolation, Jeanette began creating skincare products for Mikey
made of wholesome and natural ingredients. She didn't want to bombard

his tiny body with chemicals found in many products on the market. Her hand-crafted skincare products worked wonders, and suddenly, friends and family were trying to get some of her awesome concoctions. This gave her the idea to launch a skincare product line, and Herbs and Mylk was born.

Despite the challenges of 2020, Jeanette launched her company. She had a great website and immediately started selling her small batch soaps, lotions, and her "It's a Vibe" apparel line. She sells to several boutique shops and consumers all over the country through her website.

Jeanette's brand is growing, and all it took was four things: 1) her body to do the work and make the beautiful and effective products; 2) her mind to create a business plan and social media strategy; 3) recipes created using her experience as an herbalist; and 4) her soul and love for her son and others, which led her to share her gift and inspiration with the world. Jeanette donates monthly to causes that support other sick children. Now Mikey is leading a healthy, happy life, and Jeanette is opening her first brick-and-mortar retail shop.

Exercise

1. What clean and natural product do you use regularly that helps nourish your body, mind, and soul?

   _____

   _____

   _____

2. If you were an inventor, what product would you create to aid in healing the body, mind, and soul?

_____

_____

_____

_____

_____

Challenge: Look up products and services near you that help heal the body, mind, and soul. Are you worth the investment? I think so!

Practicing a Positive Mindset

Have you ever lost your cool with your child or reacted in a way you regret? I know I have, and I feel quite terrible when it happens. This is where a positive, calm, and forgiving mindset can come into play.

Remember my story about Luca and the box of chocolates—he came into my room covered in brown stuff I momentarily thought was poop? When I picture his smiling, guilty, chocolate-smeared face and the chocolate all over the leather couch, I chuckle. However, I then feel a pang of guilt because I can still hear Luca sobbing after I yelled at him. It made me realize I am quick to anger and get annoyed over things that aren't the end of the world like messes, mistakes, and lost productivity. All of that can cause me to lose focus on what really matters: spending time with Luca. The best thing I can do is hold myself accountable, try harder to maintain my calm, and teach my son that mistakes happen and it is important to be accountable for our actions and apologize when we lose our temper.

Now whenever Luca accidently spills a drink or makes a mess, he apologizes and says, "Mistakes happen, Mommy. I will try to do better next time." I respond by telling him, "It is okay," and I ask if he will assist me with clean up duty. We also make a point at bedtime to say what we are grateful for, and it typically is spending time together or specific family members. This has become a beautiful practice and routine of ours that allows for both of us to slow down and be grateful for the blessings in our lives.

I am so proud my son is learning a positive mindset, being accountable for his actions, apologizing when called for, and understanding that he is perfectly imperfect. I pray that this will help him be successful, kind, and patient with others throughout his life.

Exercise

1. Describe a time you lost patience and responded harshly to someone you love. How did you feel?

    _____

    _____

    _____

    _____

    _____

2. How will you work to curb your anger in the future?

Challenge: Luca and I often practice snake breaths when he or I get mad, frustrated, or just can't turn off our minds before bed. I challenge you to try doing the snake breath at least once each day whenever you start to feel angry, frustrated, or overtired. Breathe in deeply; when you exhale, do so slowly while hissing like a snake.

Seeking Professionals

I believe in the stories in this chapter and the importance of healing the body, mind, and soul so much, but I also know this chapter's topic is much bigger than what I have covered and the expertise I am qualified to offer. Everyone has had some sort of trauma, pain, or health issue. Some of us have had fewer problems, but we have all experienced some or many issues and setbacks.

Various ways exist to cope with our experiences. Some coping methods that people take are toxic, some hinge on avoidance, and others face things head on. Whether you are grieving a loss, need healing from a childhood or recent trauma, struggle with an addiction, or have a toxic relationship, help is near. We live in a world with access to many professional services and individuals trained to give you the gift of healing.

Before I was an adult, I hadn't dabbled in or understood many of the alternative healing ideas below. However, now that I have experienced the physical and mental trauma of childbirth and pregnancy, I found the courage to seek help. I have sought out many services that have ended up being very beneficial to my health and wellbeing.

I worked with a therapist to curb postpartum depression, saw a homeopathic doctor for my Hashimoto's disease, a chiropractor to adjust my spine, a massage therapist (which I also use as an opportunity to meditate), a physical therapist for pelvic floor therapy, a marriage counselor to combat the marital rollercoaster, and a personal trainer to strengthen my sore mom bod. I also experienced Reiki, a psychic reading, and tarot card readings, and I consulted my pastor for support. Other valuable resources are available such as grief and addiction counselors, acupuncturists, dieticians, support groups, nutritionists, mainstream physicians, and psychologists.

I hope this chapter helps you start a conversation with yourself and sets you on a journey to heal your body, mind, and soul. Just know that one size does not fit all, and don't put a time limit on healing yourself—we all have different journeys, and everyone's journey is sacred. Remember, seeking out resources to help achieve optimal health is not weakness. It takes great courage to be honest about our thoughts, physical condition, and spiritual wellbeing. Be open to the abundant resources available, and seek out healing opportunities because you deserve to feel whole.

Exercise

1. What area of your life needs work? What three things can you do in the next thirty days to heal your body, mind, and soul?

    _____

    _____

    _____

    _____

2. If money were not an excuse, what would your self-care monthly routine look like? Find a way to work toward this and invest in your health.

    _____

    _____

    _____

    _____

Summary

Take care of yourself, accept yourself, and heal yourself first and foremost. Love is hard to give if we don't love ourselves. Self-care, nurturing relationships, and unplugging are essential to a happy and healthy life. Then, and only then, can you take care of, accept, and love others. Accept and understand that our bodies are temples and need to function a certain way to reach a heightened state of mind and happiness. Seek out what you need to be healthy.

AMANDA MOTTOLA

CHAPTER 20
PUSHING THE LIMITS

"Success is no accident. It is hard work, perseverance, learning, studying, sacrifice, and most of all, love of what you are doing or learning to do."

— Pelé

In the last chapter, we talked about healing the mind, body, and soul, which is vital to success and happiness. Now we will reflect on everything you have read and the exercises you completed so you can prepare to move toward the future you deserve. Together, let's move forward, push the limits, and be who we are meant to be.

Honoring the Past for the Future

Have you considered what your *why* is and how you want to be remembered when you are gone?

Death is a grim reminder that no matter where we start or where we go, we all have the same destination, regardless of how hard we try to keep time bottled up. Life is an ever-moving force that keeps its momentum even after we are gone.

Pete's grandfather, Alfred, passed away the day after Mother's Day in 2013.

He was ninety-one, and like my grandparents, he lived a long life of love and family. Even though I was not related to him officially at the time, in the five years leading up to his death, I had seen him about once a month and considered him a third grandfather. His words were wise and comforting. He always told us the best life advice he could give us was to never get old and *pazienza, pazienza, pazienza* (be patient)—you say it three times, so it sticks.

I feel, as a society, we take time for granted, so visits with Alfred were always a reminder to slow down, take time to smell the roses, and most of all, be patient. Our visits became routine, and, in some respects, I took them for granted. He was old and wasn't drinking from the fountain of youth, at least not that I knew of. I knew his "never get old" advice was impossible, but I am a the-glass-is-half-full type, so I think the fountain of youth may exist. If you know the coordinates, please direct message me when you can!

Before Grandpa Alfred's decline, I had never watched someone dying in front of me. It was incredibly sobering and put me face to face with the reality of the circle of life. And emotions and fears about mortality I didn't know existed surfaced.

I find myself at times clinging to materialistic things like money, fame, fortune, etc. because they are tangible and make sense to my conscious brain. It can be scary and upsetting to consider our mortality, but when reflecting on the past and looking toward the future, it is important to be realistic and accepting of our outcome in addition to preventatively planning for those you would be leaving behind someday. You would be surprised how many adults don't have wills. Not having plans made prior to our final days can lead a problematic and stressful mess for those we leave behind to clean things up. So make sure to plan accordingly and wisely; nobody wants to be dealing with probate and other issues while grieving.

Ultimately, none of the tangible things or accolades we earn in life are transferrable beyond the grave, so we must make the most of our time here on Earth. And while we are at it, we should put the best interest of children at the forefront of our thoughts and actions since the future of humanity depends on them.

I like to have a present and past *why* because it keeps me grounded and determined to plow forward through rain or shine and push the limits. Like Sara Blakely says, our *why* should be bigger than just us, and I couldn't agree more because that is when magic starts happening. My present *why* is centered on life's many blessings. More specifically, my little planet with my two Mottola boys and my husband Peter. I will be successful and make the world a better place for them and the future generations that come after me. *Pazienza, pazienza, pazienza* until the day I die.

Exercise

1. What sparks joy in you, and does it align with your current lifestyle?

   _____

   _____

   _____

   _____

2. How do you want to be remembered?

_____

_____

_____

_____

Managing Cyber Overload

In the cyber age, it is so easy to get caught up in keeping up with the Joneses. Friends and friends of friends post amazing pictures of vacations, cars, homes, etc. sometimes making us feel less than.

Let's start with the easiest mindset tweak. *Stop* comparing yourself to these seemingly larger-than-life people because all that glitters is not gold. Plus, I'm 95 percent sure you have a great life or *could* have a great life when you are ready for it. If you aren't experiencing adventure, fun, and wealth, it may just come down to your mindset and how you allocate your time, energy, and money. I know, I know, it's easy to say! I, too, am guilty of taking a ride on this social media jealousy train in the woe-is-me caboose. But this ticket has no destination and just keeps going and going without getting anywhere.

Throughout history, we have found distractions to pass the time. As with anything, if we overindulge in distractions, or worse, the negativity associated with some of the distractions at our fingertips, we risk losing focus on our goals and becoming hyper-focused on what we don't want.

Do you have some sort of mental or physical bucket list of things you want to do and places you want to go? If you don't, I highly recommend creating one because it can help you be more intentional about how you spend your time. Remember, it's always good to put dreams and goals out into the universe because you will then be held accountable for them and you will, in my experience, then move toward them.

Your goals don't have to be extravagant. But go wild with me with the following goals based on my personal bucket list:

- Build my dream house
- Have babies (Luca and Enzo and more to come!)
- Find my birth mom (Completed August 2015)
- Backpack through Italy (Completed September 2017)
- Own a soccer club
- See a Steelers game in Pittsburgh
- Check out Tennessee's music scene
- Go to every zoo in the US (I can check off CT, NY, PA, RI so far)
- Go on a safari
- Sponsor an orphanage in South America
- Sponsor an annual mission trip

Exercise

1. Give yourself the gift of no digital distraction and unplug. Ignore the internet for an entire weekend. On Monday, write down what you did and how it felt.

_____

_____

_____

_____

2. Create a bucket list or revisit an old bucket list.

_____

_____

_____

_____

Surviving Against the Odds

Emily Crabtree is a friend of mine and a survivor. She has been fighting bone cancer since 2002 when a tumor in her femur was discovered. She was in college at the time and has undergone ninety months of chemo and six lung surgeries.

Despite Emily's body and mind surviving what has been an ultramarathon of health challenges, she is still a positive, kind, and motivated woman. Although Emily doesn't always have the physical strength to do everything she wants to do, she finds ways to contribute to causes that are important to her. It is not uncommon for Emily to spearhead fund raising and have a slew of doctors, nurses, friends, and family rally to her side to support the cause in any way they can.

Emily has been cancer-free since 2019 and attributes much of her success in fighting cancer to the doctors and care she gets at the Rush Cancer Center. Emily says, "Half the battle is trusting in the care you are getting and knowing you are in the right place, and I am in the right place at Rush."

Emily is also in the right place in the world. She works for the Children's Tumor Foundation as the senior director of development operations, helping to execute countless events and fundraisers. She brightens the day of anyone who is lucky enough to know or work with her.

Exercise

1. How has the health hurdle of yourself or someone close to you impacted your life?

   _____

   _____

   _____

2. How can you show up for someone who is currently sick or having a hard time?

   _____

   _____

   _____

Quick Thinking for the Win

They say you can't fit a square peg into a round hole. I say you sure can; you just need a lathe. I have and will always refuse to aimlessly follow, even though there is a sense of security when we fall in line and skip down the path with everyone else. I like to march to the beat of my own bodhran, think differently, and be an innovator.

When selecting a wedding band to complement my engagement ring, I wanted something special and perfect for me. I ended up going with a band enhancer that had a round setting for my princess cut engagement ring. I liked the look of two different metals together, so I went with a platinum and rose gold band enhancer.

Four years after our wedding, the diamond popped out of my engagement ring. I brought it to the jeweler, who explained it would continue to happen because the tension of the round setting against the square princess cut was weakening the metal. I asked about my options. He said I could get a new wedding band, or we could fuse the band enhancer to my engagement ring. I declined because I really didn't want to make it harder to clean all the crevices in the ring, and I knew I might want to pair either the enhancer or engagement ring with a different ring in the future. Even if I had to fix it again, it would be okay.

The wedding band story is an example of how I like to be different and make decisions for myself. I also want to tell you about a time when I thought I had messed up royally but keeping my wits and having a positive mindset saved the day.

I was interviewing for a job at Avid Marketing Group, a marketing agency that specialized in alcoholic beverages. This was the first time I interviewed with three people at one time for a job, which was a bit intimidating. I talked with the managing partner DeAnna Drapeau, vice president Jonathan Zawrotny, and Laura Balinskas who would be my boss. I smiled, continued to breathe deeply, and made eye contact. Drapeau looked at my resume and noticed I had written Diego when I meant Diageo. It was one of their biggest accounts.

As she looked up at me, I smiled, embarrassed, and said I had been working on my Spanish and didn't catch the typo. I explain I was adopted from Paraguay and really hoped one day to go down to find my birth family. This explanation and story diffused a situation that could have cost me the job and turned my typo into laughs from all three interviewers. The conversation then shifted to my adoption and what makes Amanda Marie special.

The interview continued for another fifty minutes after my typo *faux pas*. At one point, Zawrotny asked if I was a quick thinker. Without hesitation, I said, "Yes, I like to think I am." He quickly followed up with, "Why is a manhole cover round?" I breathed and said, "Well, a manhole cover is round because if it was square it wouldn't fit." He smiled and said, "Hum, great answer. No one has said that before."

Within a day or so, I got the job, and I was able to pack my mind with an arsenal of beverage alcohol law knowledge, program activation dos and don'ts, and management dos and don'ts that I am forever grateful for. I also learned that it pays to be honest, authentic, and different.

I have gone through life refusing to follow the crowd. I am living proof that you can bounce back from mistakes, overcome mental and physical hurdles, and come out on top.

Exercise

1. Describe one of your worst job interviews. What advice would you have given yourself before that interview?

   _____

   _____

   _____

   _____

2. How have you used wit or quick problem solving to recover from a mistake?

   _____

   _____

   _____

   _____

Dribbling Forward

While writing this final chapter, I had the privilege and honor to catch up with the one and only John Paul Vincent "Sonny" Vaccaro, the godfather of basketball sneakers. To my delight, the conversation did not disappoint. This self-made man refers to himself as Italian-centric and Pittsburgh proud. We hit it off because my adoptive family is from the Pittsburgh area, so I am well-versed in all that is Pittsburghese, especially the sports scene— Go Steelers, Penguins, and Pirates! Also, Italian food and people will always have a place in my heart.

Vaccaro began his life in Trafford Township, Pennsylvania. The son of Italian immigrants, he didn't have the financial resources to attend college, so he needed a sports scholarship to get the education he dreamed of. He was on a football scholarship until he got injured. When one door closes, always another opens. Youngstown State University gave him a scholarship and he got a second chance. Yet again, he got hurt and his athletic career ended before it had started, but these setbacks didn't stop him from getting his degree and finding success.

Vaccaro founded several grassroot basketball blockbuster events. His first major event was the Dapper Dan Roundball Classic, America's original high school All-Star Classic he co-founded in Pittsburgh in 1965. The most widely imitated event in prep basketball, this charitable classic annually brought together the twenty-two most-gifted high school all-stars in the country, and it holds the all-time attendance record for a high school all-star event. From 1984 through 2006, the annual ABCD Camp held each July was a prestigious event. For twenty-three years, the ABCD Camp showcased the next wave of outstanding players for scouts and coaches. Students who attended his camps and all-star games included Kobe Bryant,

Lebron James, Derrick Rose, Kevin Garnett, and Shaquille O'Neal.

In 1990, Vaccaro also established the non-profit organization Hoops That Help with an inaugural event organized in partnership with Comic Relief (founded by Billy Crystal, Whoopi Goldberg, and Robin Williams) at the Superdome in New Orleans. This match-up featured LSU vs Notre Dame and set an attendance record of 63,000 fans at a regular season game. Contributions have surpassed $4 million over the years for programs benefitting the homeless, AIDS education, The Boys and Girls Clubs, and other charities.

Throughout the years and to this day, Sonny regularly makes appearances on television and radio sports programs all over the country. His to-the-point, no-nonsense perspectives have led to countless media outlets and organizations seeking him out, including *60 Minutes*, HBO's *Real Sports*, *CBS Evening News*, PBS's *Frontline*, *On the Record with Bob Costas*, ABC *Nightline*, *Good Morning America*, and ESPN's *Outside the Lines*.

One of his campers once asked, "Sonny, why don't they make tennis shoes that can be worn on and off the court?" Vaccaro pondered the question but had no answer. Vaccaro did not know then that this simple question would change the relationship between sports and the shoe industry and change the future of basketball marketing. Vaccaro went on to play a big role at companies like Nike, Reebok, and Adidas.

According to an article by *USA Today*, Vaccaro encouraged Nike to invest in Michael Jordan to get a foothold in basketball. Michael Jordan was not the number-one draft pick. Some dispute the credit or parts of how this deal played out, but regardless, Vaccaro's charisma and love for basketball were paramount in signing Michael Jordan.

Through his exciting journey, Vaccaro has learned a lot about life and basketball. He has three important lessons to share.

Sonny Vaccaro's Three Important Life Lessons:

1: **BELIEVE** in your talent and role in this world. Many will try to shake your confidence and challenge your capabilities, but the key is to never lose sight that you can succeed. Stay true to yourself and you can do whatever you want—just believe it's in you and start—you can get there if you seriously work at it.

2: **FOLLOW** your drive. Don't worry about all the thoughts that bounce around your head. When something clicks in your mind and tells you that *this is a good idea*, take notice and focus on the "good ideas" that keep coming back to you; those are the keepers. Don't shut your mind off and let the detours and distractions and naysayers derail you from acting *on the good ideas*.

3: **ADVANCE** your game with relentless determination—but be ready to adjust the course. Where you are at each given point might not be where you are meant to be. If you feel like you need to change paths or create something new for yourself, then be ready for the opportunity. All your progress, every small step that helps you develop a new capability or benchmark in reaching your ultimate goal, is the way to achieve your best life.

Vaccaro's determination to believe he could do something with his life has provided him with the opportunity to advocate for economic opportunities under the law for athletes of all ages and make a difference in the world of basketball and beyond.

One game-changing example is the *O'Bannon vs. NCAA* litigation, which has had momentous implications for the future of collegiate sports and the athletes that play. This case upholds the rights of players to retain ownership of their images subsequent to their participation in collegiate athletics. Sonny was a catalyst in this case and acted as an unpaid consultant for Hausfeld LLP.

His ability to pinpoint and run with the "good ideas" and his stellar business instincts have served him well. He has not only revolutionized the basketball world, but he advanced his life in a way that is meaningful and paves the way for others to follow their own intuition. He currently lives on the West Coast and enjoys life with his lovely wife Pam while continuing to follow sports marketing updates, prospects at various levels, and initiatives that benefit the rights of athletes and the future of American basketball.

Exercise

1. Which of Vaccaro's three lessons resonate with you?

    _____

    _____

    _____

    _____

2. If you could attend any final sporting event, which would it be?

_____

_____

_____

_____

3. Describe your favorite pair of shoes.

_____

_____

_____

_____

Summary

We face many negative things and find many reasons to get stuck in grief, self-absorption, sadness, and hardships. But those times are, in fact, the most important. They offer a chance to break free and embrace a positive mindset focused on the things that bring us joy, like spending time with loved ones and doing the things we love to do.

Frank Sinatra said, "I would like to be remembered as a man who had a wonderful time living life, a man who had good friends, fine family—and I don't think I could ask for anything more than that, actually." Every decision, mistake, failure, and success works to shape our future and our legacy. Live like tomorrow is not guaranteed—no excuses, no complaints. Life is going to keep on coming no matter what, and we only have so much time to get what we are meant to done. So, take a deep breath, prioritize, and move forward.

Never stop living and pushing the limits. Live the way you want to be remembered.

AMANDA MOTTOLA

A FINAL NOTE
ENTERING THE FUTURE LIKE A BOSS

"There are two types of people who will tell you that you
cannot make a difference in this world: those who are
afraid to try and those who are afraid you will succeed."

— Ray Goforth

Congratulations! You read the whole book. It has been a rollercoaster
of journeys merging into one epic compilation. The years, months,
weeks, and days will continue ticking by, so be the most productive and
fulfilled person you possibly can be. You deserve to reach your goals and
make the most of each of your days. If you have breath in your lungs, it is
a beautiful day and an opportunity to inspire others and get closer to your
path. Life is meant to be enjoyed.

Even though I have not walked a mile in your shoes, I have felt pain and
been knocked out by life a few times, as have the many inspiring individuals featured in this book. It is one thing to attend a conference or event, or
read a motivational book and get hyped up. It is another to keep the positive words, motivation, and experience from dissipating over time.

Now that you have finished reading this book, are you going to put this book
on the bookshelf and not take action toward a better life? Or are you going

to act on your dreams, goals, and visions using many of the strategies, techniques, and suggestions to implement them? I am challenging you to kick off your better choices and create a new, improved you now. Don't wait for the new year or some future date. I know you have it in you to keep the momentum you are feeling right now going because you picked up this book and learned about my journey, you learned about the journey of others featured in this book, and you discovered things about your own journey.

> "In life you have to keep doing what you believe. You have to ask yourself do you really want this from your heart. Is it for the self-glory or is it for something bigger? Sometimes the idea you come up with may seem impossible to the rest of the world but that doesn't mean it is impossible to you. And if you can inspire one or two people in a good way then you can inspire the world."
>
> — Purja, Mountaineer

I encourage you to write out and create ten actionable steps you can commit to doing within the next ninety days.

1. _____

2. _____

3. _____

4. _____

5. _____

6. _____

7. _____

8. _____

9. _____

10. _____

In this book, you learned about overcoming insecurities, taking risks, finding joy, mentoring minds, embracing your mistakes, empowering your soul, feeding your entrepreneurial spirit, kissing the bully goodbye, climbing mountains, creating your own destiny, and evolving through family changes. Most importantly, you learned that everything you do drives you forward, and even though we spend years studying to be someone or do something, sometimes that something just doesn't feel right. Life may have something bigger in store for you. If you feel compelled to change paths or create something, do so. Ultimately, you are who you are, so stay true to your core self. You can do whatever you want—just believe it, start it, and do it with all your heart. If you find what lights you up inside, you will thrive.

I wish you good fortune, peace, and happiness as your journey continues to unfold. Keep following the greenlights, the lit-up paths, and the universe's push to be all you can be! Continue to learn because life is full of opportunities, and learning is truly a lifelong journey. I hope you enjoy the ride!

Amanda Mottola

AMANDA MOTTOLA

ABOUT THE AUTHOR

Hola! I was born in Asuncion, Paraguay, and I was adopted by an American family—the Doerrs. I grew up in Milford, Connecticut, and attended the Academy of our Lady of Mercy Lauralton Hall. I attended Manhattanville College for a year and finished my bachelor's at the University of New Haven. I am the CEO of Otraway, a marketing agency based in New England; CEO of Freestyle Football Club, a professional freestyle soccer booking agency; and a speaker, mindset coach, and entrepreneur. I enjoy being immersed in other cultures, food, and language. I also enjoy a dry cabernet, a bold coffee, listening to and telling stories, antiquing, watching *Shark Tank* as a family, dancing to music, and road trips to new destinations. I have an intense love for people and spend a lot of time helping others and making the community a better place. Naturally, the fall is my favorite time of the year because it is jam-packed with holidays and family time.

Family, community, and the American Dream are everything to me. I currently live in Rhode Island with my husband Pete and two sons Luca and Enzo.

AMANDA MOTTOLA COACHING

I encourage you to contact me and tell me what you liked about my book, what you disliked, or what you felt was missing so I can improve it for future readers. But more importantly, I want to know you, what makes you tick, and what obstacles and adversities you have faced or are currently up against. Are you unsure of your next move or trapped in an unfulfilling limbo? I am a master connector and want to help you. In fact, I want to hear from you so much that I am offering a complimentary, no-obligation thirty- to sixty-minute discovery call, Google Duo, or in-person meeting (if location allows) to see how I can assist you on you journey.

My email address is amanda@amandamottola.com and my personal cell phone number is (203) 535-5003. Due to spam blockers, the best way to reach me is through text. In your text, please tell me your name, contact info, and location. I will follow up to schedule your complimentary coaching consultation.

BOOK AMANDA MOTTOLA TO SPEAK AT YOUR NEXT EVENT

Amanda Mottola is available to speak to people of all ages at a wide variety of events from schools to corporate functions. Are you in search of a dynamic speaker to motivate your team and bring some diverse energy into the mix? Look no farther than Amanda Mottola. She has more than twelve years of corporate business experience and experience working for and with small and large nonprofits, mentoring, training, and much more. You can expect one thing from Amanda—she will inspire your audience.

For speaking inquiries, please contact Amanda Mottola at:

Amanda@AmandaMottola.com

(203) 535-5003